Point Arena

Los Angeles

Pigeon Point

Point Vicente

Point Bonita

A Sampling of
California Lightstations

Anacapa

Discovering the
California Coast

Discovering the
California

A Sunset Pictorial

Coast

LANE PUBLISHING CO., MENLO PARK, CALIFORNIA

Contents

SPECIAL FEATURES

Safeguarding the Natural Setting

Getting to Know the Coast

Maps

Selected Readings 286

Index 288

Edited by JACK MCDOWELL

Design Consultant: Cummings Walker
Maps and Endsheet Drawings: Joe Seney
Illustrations: Greg Irons

Executive Editor, Sunset Books: David E. Clark

Front Cover: Russian Gulch, Mendocino County. Back Cover:
Beach, Santa Barbara. Title Page: Sonoma County shore.

Unless otherwise noted, all photographs are by
Jack McDowell.

This book was printed and bound by Graphic Arts Center,
Portland, Oregon, from litho film prepared by them. Body
type is Helvetica; type for heads is Helvetica and Americana
Black, composed by Haber Typographers, Inc., New York.
Paper for pages is Enamel, made by Westvaco, Luke, Maryland.

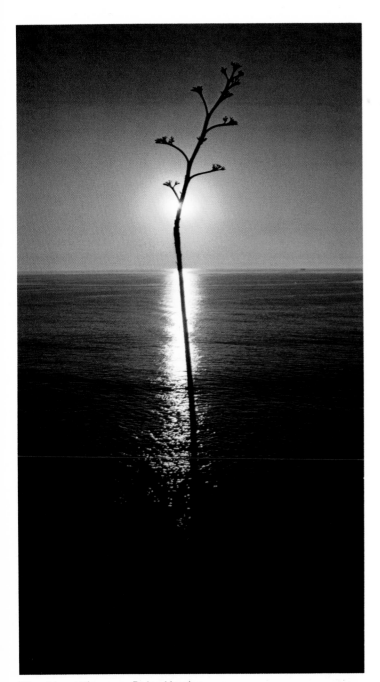

Weed in setting sun, Palos Verdes

California's

California's western edge is alive! Drive for a few miles on the sinuous coast highway, taking in a comprehensive view, or stroll a length of shore, inspecting the endless variations in sea and sand. Every inch is active, pulsating. Changing slowly under the natural processes of the earth or being altered quickly with man's works, the coast is more than a static collection of places. It is a dynamic entity.

For 1,100 miles up and down the state stretches the coast of California, spreading out from the water's edge to encompass offshore islands as well as seaward slopes of the westernmost mountains. The coast is a zone of unique geologic structures, life forms, climates. It is a valuable natural resource, a place for recreation, solitude, study. For those first experiencing California, seeing its coast can be an exhilarating discovery. For those who know the state well, realizing what the coast really is and what it could become is an enlightening *re*discovery.

SHAPING OF THE SHORE

Like California's people, its coast is youthful. Wave-cut terraces that rise in great steps from the shoreline indicate geologically recent

Headland near Trinidad

Rock island, Crescent City

Western Edge

Place of Land and Sea

Sand beach, Laguna Beach

Forested slopes near Mendocino

uplifts in the earth's crust, drops in sea level, or combinations of the two processes. At present the shore appears to be stable or slowly subsiding, as evidenced by cliffs formed by prolonged wave action at the same level.

Because waves come from the ocean, the sea is chief architect of the coast, and when sea meets land, the latter can only react defensively. In one place it folds or faults upward; in another it accumulates sediments to extend itself. But always the forces of waves, wind, and rain cause the land to give way.

The Pacific is the most active natural force at work along California's shore. Nevertheless, the substance of the earth determines just how the shore will be shaped. In the north, waves pound at rocky headlands—picking at stony cliffs to dig deep caverns and coves, sculpting arches that collapse to leave bold sea stacks. Chunks of land are pulverized and deposited in coastal indentations where they form pocket beaches as the sea endeavors to straighten the sawtooth shore.

Below Point Conception, though, the east-swinging coastline undergoes dramatic changes. Here, sand-laden currents flow along the shoreline, smoothing it and laying down an almost unbroken curve of wide beach. Cliffs are still present, but they stand back from the water. It's as if they were tamed in spirit as well as in form by the sea that gnaws them, the civilization that crowds them.

Thistle heads, Palos Verdes

THE NATURAL WORLD

Just as the sea physically changes the shore, so does it create numerous other coastal conditions collectively known as "environment." Tending to cool much of the north, the powerful California current neglects to turn Point Conception's corner. As a result, warmer waters in the south radiate their influence landward. Here, temperate-climate species of plants and animals approach the southern limits of their range, mixing with semitropical species reaching their northern boundaries.

Differences are apparent all along the coast. To the far north, winter rains and summer fogs nourish redwoods, firs, and spruce, and a system of streams and rivers flourishes. Around the Golden Gate, signs of dryness appear. Chaparral covers many slopes; rivers become fewer, finally giving way to seasonal streams. Breathtaking as its landscape is, California's coast possesses even more valuable natural resources: forests in the north, oil in the south, and a wealth of wildlife in between. Estuaries and wetlands teem with migratory fowl, shore birds, spawning fish, and organisms essential to the natural food chain. Offshore kelp beds harbor entire colonies of marine life. Otters, seals, and sea lions gambol in the surf. Rocky pools form a natural aquarium for small creatures dependent on the rise and fall of the tides.

BOB EVANS

Sea lions, San Miguel Island

Fish in kelp, Monterey

10

Gulls, Long Beach

Feeding pelicans, Anacapa Island

THE PRESENCE OF MAN

For hundreds of years man's presence scarcely disturbed this coastal environment. But in the last half-century, greater wealth, more leisure, and sheer population pressures have subjected the California coast to the often destructive influence of civilization. From north to south, the general trend is a shifting from rural (even primitive) regions to increasingly urban ones. Spreading centers of intense development are evidence that many miles of shore have been usurped from nature's proprietorship.

The damage caused by man's presence has not been light, and the list of his transgressions against nature can be recited with what is, by now, a tired familiarity. Sewage outfalls and discharged wastes foul beaches and estuaries. Industrial and agricultural contaminants threaten the ability of shore birds and mammals to reproduce. Oil spills stain the sands and kill unknown numbers of creatures. The sight of oil rigs defiles many beaches and offshore waters.

Deluded by the same false picture of plenty that caused the gray whale to be hunted to the edge of oblivion, man overfishes the coastal waters and strips the tidal lands. He fills and develops thousands of acres of wetlands, seriously shrinking vital wildlife habitats and

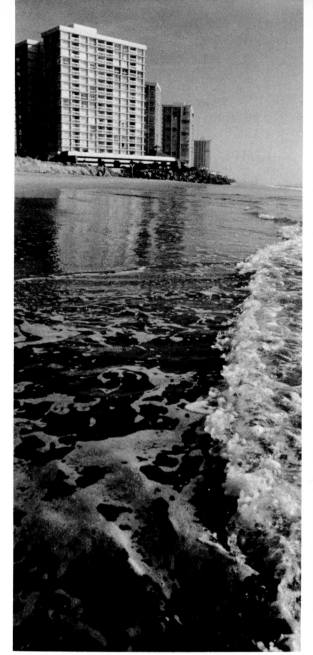

Condominium, Coronado Island, San Diego

endangering or eradicating many species. He covers agricultural land with residential and industrial structures. He dams and diverts rivers, cutting off the major sand supply of beaches. He builds obstructions such as break-waters, which further disturb sand transport and cause stripping of the shore.

In rural areas many problems are created by mismanagement of resources—land erosion frequently results from improper timber cutting.

Populated areas have their own share of troubles caused by sheer overcrowding: traffic jams, full parking lots, and packed strands are often the summer weekend norm. Blocking what should rightfully be everyone's view are omnipresent highrise buildings. Poorly planned housing sited on unstable bluffs causes earth slumping and property damage. Landowners wishing to protect a bit of shore from misuse—or anxious to preserve their privacy—post "no trespassing" signs and erect fences, denying public access to the shore.

DEFENDING THE COAST

Grievous though it is, man's record is not all bad. Enlightened voices have spoken in the past against reckless exploitation, and such precious resources as Torrey pines, gray whales,

Sheep ranch, Mendocino County

Home, Bodega Bay

Sign, Big Sur coast

State Route 1, Mendocino County

and sea otters have been protected. Parks have been established to preserve important parcels of land. Man is realizing that to tilt the delicate balance in one place is to cause a train of disruption that circles back to directly affect his life. He is learning that the concept of limitless wealth is a false one.

Increasingly, conservation-minded individuals and groups have rallied to the coast's defense. In late 1975 the California Coastal Zone Conservation Commission—created in 1972 by statewide referendum—offered to the legislature a master plan for coastal use. The plan's stated aims are to preserve the coast for the benefit of present and future generations and to allow it to meet human needs in a manner that safeguards its natural integrity.

The issues raised are thorny. For example, public access to the shore is accepted as of primary importance. But how can this principal be judiciously applied to allow everyone to use the shore without denying the individual the experiences of solitude? And how can the needs of civilization be accommodated so as not to conflict with the processes of nature? Regardless of what the plan is and how it is implemented, questions like these will continue to exist.

It's more than a scenic world of waves and sunsets, this California coast. It is a living world in constant transition, a vital resource that demands to be respected and deserves to be discovered.

13

The North

The Remote Shore—The Lack of

There's no sharp demarcation line, no sign pointing seaward. But in the north, California's long coast begins properly at the Oregon border. Just below the quarantine station, spray blown inland from Pelican Beach whips across U.S. 101, the well-traveled roadway linking those few lonely settlements spotted along this remote shore.

Farthest north of California's coastal towns, Smith River is a pastoral focus of dairying and flower growing. From the foothills to the sea, fields are given over to slim Easter lilies or fat cattle. Smith River sits a couple of miles inland from Pelican Bay, but Crescent City—to the south—overlooks the Pacific Ocean, and this town's island-dotted inshore waters evoke memories of a Japanese painting.

Below Crescent City the highway swings eastward, slipping in and out of Redwood National Park's majestic groves, twisting past Klamath (self-styled salmon capital of the world), and sweeping through Orick, southern terminus of Redwood Park. Though sometimes losing sight of the sea, the road is never far from water in this river-and-stream country.

Beyond Big Lagoon and not far below Patrick's Point State Park, the colorful fishing settlement of Trinidad perches high on a coastal bluff reached by a turnoff from the main road. Close by the highway, comes Arcata, followed by hustling, bustling Eureka. Then U.S. 101 leaves the northern shore, bending far inland as if fearful of the scenic but formidable bulge comprising the jagged hills of Mattole River country and the ragged peaks of the King Range.

Coast

People is its Greatest Charm

There is rapture on the lonely
   shore;
There is society, where none intrudes
By the deep sea, and music in its
   roar:
I love not Man the less, but Nature more.
                              —Lord Byron

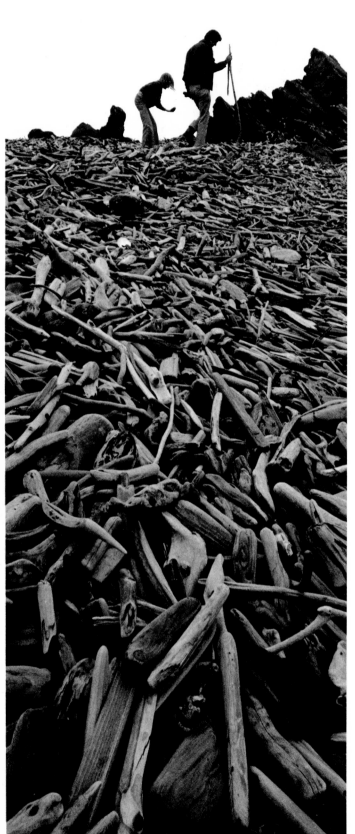

Getting the DRIFT on the unspoiled SHORE

"I like pieces of wood that look like animals," declared the lady from Sacramento, whose high-heeled shoes were fastened to her feet with rubber bands so they wouldn't come off in the sand. "I take them home and set them out in the yard for decoration."

"I'm on pension," said the old gentleman, pausing in his brisk hike along Crescent City's shoreline. "Every morning I walk the beaches and pick up stuff to sell to shops in town."

Seaside visitors are intrigued by finds of flotsam cast up by the ocean. Happily they fill auto trunks with branches and gnarled roots that have been carried downriver from inland forests. Seaside residents are used to having such wrack deposited almost at their doorstep but are no less enthralled by the forms sculpted by wave and weather.

After the kind of November storm that drags drift from one beach to another, shells, gemstones, and mysterious bits of bone strew the sand—all treasures for the earnest beachcomber. Glass floats—some as large as basketballs—sometimes turn up. A lucky find is a drifter, a disc of yellow plastic put into the sea by the Coast and Geodetic Survey to track currents.

NO PROBLEM OF SCARCITY
Knowledgeable beachcombers canvass coves and scrutinize inlets daily, since wave action and tidal movements rearrange such mountains of drift, bringing to light ever-new treasures in wood.

KNOWING WHAT TO LOOK FOR
Worn smooth by friction of sand and wash of waves, glistening beach pebbles attract rockhounds from afar. Jade, opal, and agate are occasionally turned up, as are deceptive bits of colored glass. It takes a practiced eye to spot gemstones in a handful of gravel.

**EASTER LILIES,
AND A LOW-TIDE MUSEUM**
*Cool, moist climate of Smith River—
California's northernmost coastal community
—is ideal for lily culture, below. More than five
million bulbs are shipped annually to
markets throughout United States and
Canada. Weather sometimes isolates
Crescent City's Battery Point lighthouse,
above— a historical museum. Though just
200 yards from shore, it can be reached only
at low tide by walking across the reef.*

We don't have a lot of TOWNS... we've got just ENOUGH

Few in number and populated by independent, individualistic people are the north coast towns. Smith River: "Easter Lily Capital of the World," in the heart of dairy country. Crescent City: Seat of Del Norte County, home of Redwood National Park Headquarters (whose offices are built on tall pilings against a possible repetition of the disastrous tidal wave of 1964). Requa and Klamath: On the banks of Klamath River, famed for its salmon and steelhead runs. Trinidad: Commercial and sport fishing center of the north. Arcata: Home of Humboldt State College. Eureka: Seat of Humboldt County, lumber and shipping center since 1850.

In the words of a lifelong north coaster: "These are good places to live. We don't have many towns up here ... we've got just enough."

OLDEST TOWN ON THE NORTH COAST
Settled as a port in 1850 and incorporated two years later, Trinidad served as a whaling station, later as a lumber shipping point. Today the big interest is in fishing, and commercial as well as private craft crowd the picturesque harbor.

SUNDAY SOCIALIZING
*Friends come calling on a
lazy afternoon at Blue Lake,
northeast of Arcata in the
heart of the coast's
logging country.*

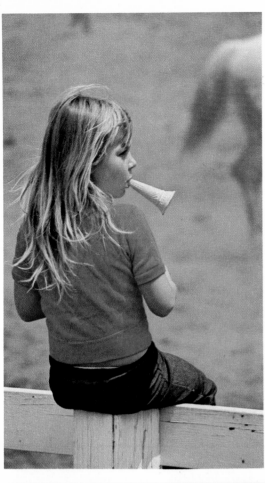

SUMMER SUN, SUMMER FUN
*Rodeo at Orick, above, salmon barbecue at
Arcata, below, mark high spots in circle of the
north country seasons. Other annual events
in Del Norte and Humboldt Counties include
All Indian Basketball Competition, Old
Timer's Day, Crab Races, Rabbit Show,
Horseshoe Pitching Meet, and, of course,
the county fairs.*

"Come on up, the FISHING'S fine"

There's no thrill like that of hooking a rod-bending, record-breaking salmon or netting a wildly wriggling trout. Because some of the state's finest fishing streams empty into the Pacific, their waters—and the inshore waters of the ocean—are happy hunting grounds for anglers of all persuasions. Seasonally teeming with salmon, trout, rockfish, and surf fish, the rivers, bays, lagoons, and deep sea make the north coast a place where all the fishing action is.

The people of the north coast are unselfish about their bounty. "Come on up," they say. "The fishing's fine."

HOIST HIM HIGH!
When salmon are really running, fishermen work the river mouths elbow to elbow. On occasion, tempers flare and someone may be hit with a wild oar, but usually there are enough fish for everyone.

*KEEP AN EYE
ON THE OCEAN
Under an in-rolling wave goes the dip net.
When lifted, it may contain ten or
fifteen pounds of silvery smelt. The wise
smelt dipper watches the surf line, ever alert
for the big wave that might dump him.*

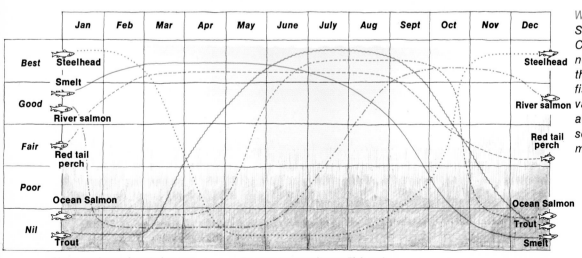

	Jan	Feb	Mar	Apr	May	June	July	Aug	Sept	Oct	Nov	Dec
Best	Steelhead											Steelhead
	Smelt											
Good												River salmon
	River salmon											
Fair	Red tail perch											Red tail perch
Poor												
	Ocean Salmon											Ocean Salmon
Nil												Trout
	Trout											Smelt

*WHEN THE FISHING'S FINE
Some of the best angling in
California is found along the
north coast. Though
the hottest time for catching
fish depends on a host of
variables, the chart
at left indicates best
seasons for hooking the
more popular species.*

**Clams are best taken during low
spring tides; crabs are best
taken December to June.**

**Be sure to consult your Fish and
Game regulations regarding
licenses, seasons, limits.**

23

DOWN IT COMES!
Chips fly as a chain saw chews through a fir, and the faller makes ready to leap clear in the event the tree kicks back as it drops. Skill and potential hazard make fallers highest paid men in woods.

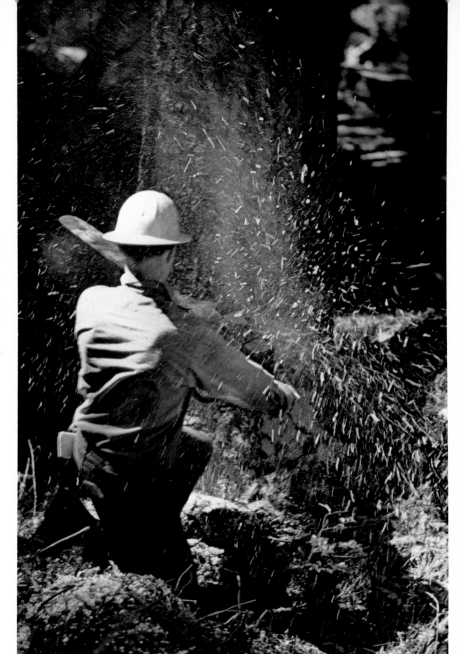

UP IT GOES!
Mammoth claw-front loader is overbalanced by mammoth redwood log. By skill and sheer mechanical power, the operator will maneuver the log closer to his machine and over their common center of gravity, then lift it high for loading onto a flatbed truck.

The
TRACK
of the cat, from
FALLER
to sawyer

The gold rush started it. Though some coastal logging began in the late 1700s, the big boom came 50 years later when it looked as if San Francisco were here to stay.

Historically, timber has been harvested by two basic methods. Selective cutting is a thinning-out process in which larger trees are removed and smaller ones left for future growth. Clearcutting—harvesting all timber in an area—is done when an entire stand of trees is mature or declining.

Downed trees are sawed—or bucked—into manageable lengths, which are then skidded through the woods by "cat" for loading onto flatbed trucks.

At the mill, friction drums, air hammers, pronged blades, or high-pressure water jets strip bark from the trunks. The naked-looking logs move to the headrig, where a screaming band saw slices them into thick sections called cants. Hustled along to ganged circular saws, then to edging and trimming machines, cants are cut tidily into boards. On a moving belt—the "green chain"—boards are graded according to the quality of wood, then go to the air yard for drying.

WETTING
AND WAITING
Logs stored in a "cold deck" must be kept moist to prevent fast drying out and subsequent splitting and checking. Decked timber is milled in January, February, and March, when rainy weather curtails operations in the woods.

ANOTHER DAY, ANOTHER WAY
Six span of oxen drag a string of logs over a highway made by laying tree trunks crossways. Such a track was called a skid road, a term that evolved into "skid row," meaning an area frequented by alcoholics. Early-day lumberjacks were hard drinkers.

Gunning the Tree. Balanced on a plank staging, head chopper used a gun stick (a scissors-like arrangement of jointed poles) to sight a line where he wanted tree to fall and thus to determine undercut.

Making the Undercut. Working opposite each other on side toward which tree was to fall, two choppers alternately swung away with their long-handled, double-bitted axes to make a deep undercut.

EARNING A DAY'S PAY
Woods crew takes a breather while posing solemnly for the camera. With only sharp axes, muscle power, and skill, men barked, split, and hewed logs into finished planks near the spot where the trees were felled.

Making the Backcut. With the undercut complete and the big block knocked out of the way, two men began to haul back and forth on a long saw, making the backcut on side opposite the undercut.

Dropping the Tree. As saw bit deep into tree, steel wedges were driven in behind it to relieve pressure and nudge tree into the line of fall. A successful fall dropped a tree without shattering it.

FALLING A TREE WAS NOT JUST HIT OR MISS
Around the turn of the century, larger trees were cut than are harvested now (there aren't as many big ones left), and a real giant took three or four days to drop. The trick was to have a tree land on a falling bed made from branches to keep the wood from being damaged.

Redwood National Park: Forests that Existed before Man

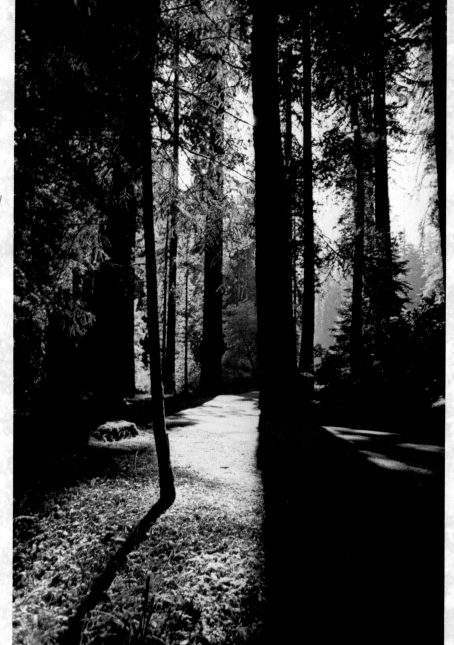

SILENCE IS GOLDEN—AND GREEN
For most of the day, sun is filtered by a dense canopy of high growth, and the forest is bathed in deep shade. In early morning and later afternoon, golden beams slant between the trunks, glowing briefly on the soft forest floor.

"Where the fog flows, the redwood grows," is an old north coast saying. And where the redwood grows is a timeless world of natural wonder.

Discovered by a Spaniard in 1769 (Don Gaspar de Portola), collected by a Scotsman in 1794 (Archibald Menzies), and named by an Austrian in 1847 (Stephan Endlicher) to honor an American Indian (Sequoya, a Cherokee), the redwood is one of California's most versatile products— and one of its most perpetually controversial subjects. Flourishing on the coast, the redwood has grown in great forests since the earth's Oligocene epoch over 30 million years ago.

Preserving a remnant of that forest—a forest that existed before the human species evolved upon the earth—is the commission of Redwood National Park.

From above Crescent City at the north to below Orick at the south, Redwood National Park is a blend of rugged coastline, deep forest, canyons, and hills. Land close to the shore is under the ocean's influence. For days at a time, thick fogs may blanket beach and bluff; temperatures are cool, rainfall heavy—all conditions to the liking of *Sequoia sempervirens*. At higher inland elevations, where summer days are hot and dry, redwoods thin out, giving way to tan oak, madrone, Douglas fir.

One of the West's greatest scenic and recreation areas, Redwood National Park is 46 miles from top to bottom, 7 miles at its greatest width. To a person not well-versed with the plan of the park, its makeup and boundaries can be somewhat confusing, for the whole comprises three state parks (Jedediah Smith, Del Norte Coast, Prairie Creek) connected by a coastal strip that, in some places, is less than half a mile wide.

SHATTERING THE STILLNESS
Of all park activities, the Great Annual Banana Slug Race, held at Prairie Creek campgrounds, is perhaps the most raucous. As spectators and prompters whoop it up, Chief Running Slug inches across the finish line into the winner's circle.

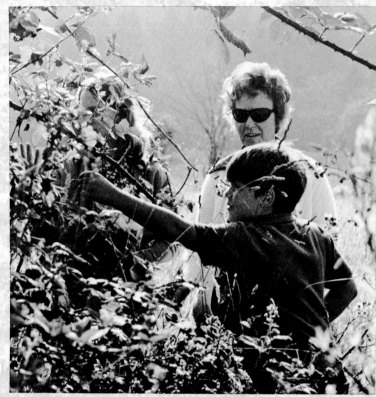

BEACHCOMBING TO BERRY PICKING
In a matter of minutes, you can stroll from a romp at water's edge, below, to a berry picking expedition inland, above. Camping, hiking, bird watching, fishing, and the opportunity for getting close to nature draw thousands of visitors to Redwood's three parks.

TOM TRACY

ONE PARK . . .
FOUR ENVIRONMENTS
Redwood National Park consists of four ecosystems
(distinct plant and animal communities): redwood forest;
marine and shore; north coastal scrub; cutover forest. Owing
to clear cutting of timber before acquisition of the land
by the Park Service, the latter environment is going through
a marked succession of changes. In a hundred years
or more, an entirely new redwood forest ecosystem will exist.

FROM THE SEA . . .
Clear of the harbor long before dawn, commercials make their ocean runs and are back to unload by early afternoon. The rest of the day is spent keeping gear in order. Long-range craft—chugging out of Eureka and Trinidad—pass weeks at sea, working as far north as Alaskan waters.

Fifteen tons of COD five tons of FLOUNDER

Surprising to even those in the fishing industry were the results of a 1971 study carried out by the California Department of Fish and Game comparing the amount of commercially caught fish in Eureka with that in San Francisco. That year, Eureka fishermen caught 30.5 million pounds of fish, in contrast to the 14 million pounds brought in by San Francisco boats. Small wonder that much of the salmon, flounder, sole, cod, and tuna sold in markets and served in restaurants farther south comes from north coast ports.

"Fifteen tons of cod . . . five tons of flounder . . ." mused the bristle-bearded trawler skipper as his catch was being unloaded. "It's hard work, but I guess a run like this makes it all okay."

. . . TO THE STORE
Four skillful swipes of a knife and fifteen seconds are all it takes to filet a cod. Packed in ice, the meat is trucked to San Francisco markets. Bones, skin, and heads— representing two-thirds of the fish—are processed as fertilizer.

EUREKA is only a gull's flight away from SAMOA

It's the largest deep water port between Portland and San Francisco, and it has two peninsulas bearing the exotic names of Samoa and Manila. Originally settled in the 1800s as a mining town, Eureka quickly grew into a major shipping center. Even when gold petered out in the northern mines, Eureka hardly noticed, because it was already flourishing from a double-barreled boom built around fishing and lumbering. Today these same themes are reflected in many ways around the city at the side of Humboldt Bay, whose waters are churned by fussy boats of the fishing fleet and ocean freighters laden with wood pulp and lumber.

The themes are echoed in the curriculum of California State College—at nearby Arcata—which offers studies in fish and game management, forestry, and oceanography.

BIG APPETITES
Once the Samoa Cookhouse fed work-hungry lumberjacks. Today it continues the tradition by dishing up all-you-can-eat breakfasts, lunches, and dinners for visitors. An accompanying museum features culinary items and tools from the early logging years.

PETER WHITELY

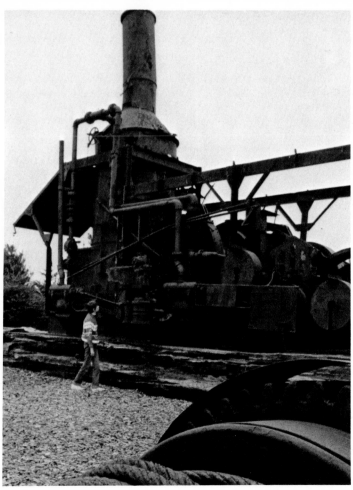

BIG SHIPS . . . AND
RELICS OF BYGONE DAYS

Everywhere apparent is Eureka's bond with the logging industry. At the edge of Humboldt Bay, stack upon stack of lumber wait for rail transport across the country or sea shipment to world ports. An earlier era of steam-operated donkey engines and locomotives is recalled at fascinating Fort Humboldt outdoor logging museum (left).

MONUMENT TO ORNAMENTATION

Bristling with gables, cupolas, and pillars, the Carson Mansion, located at Second and M Streets, is a breathtaking configuration of incised decorations, massed moldings, and carved eave boards. Constructed in 1885 by William Carson, owner of a profitable logging business, the house was occupied by three generations of his family. In 1950 the mansion was taken over by the Ingomar Club, a group of civic-minded men dedicated to preserving its heritage. The smaller Victorian across the street (right) was built by William Carson as a wedding present for one of his sons.

VICTORIAN ARCHITECTURAL TOUR
The gingerbread look began in the 1800s with the belief that the more embellishment that could be put on a building, the more beautiful it became. Turrets, towers, stained glass, and carved posts still enhance many local homes and reflect memories of a romantic style. The mapped route affords glimpses of some of the finest of Eureka's ornate structures.

THE NORTH COAST

Ferndale –
VICTORIAN VILLAGE at the crossroads of time

As if the name "Ferndale" weren't evocative enough, this pastoral town is also known as "Victorian Village" and "Cream City." Tradition is linked with all three designations.

Ferndale is the original name given to a farm that eventually grew to a community. The appellation is appropriate because of the luxuriant growth of ferns in this part of the fertile Eel River Delta. Since the same rich soil provided ideal grazing for Jersey and Guernsey cows, butter- and cream-making became an important industry. As dairying prospered, many of the farmers built large homes in the Victorian style. Some of the handsome structures remaining on large rural acreages and in town make this one of California's most picturesque settlements.

The houses of Ferndale have a well-scrubbed, well-cared-for look. The elaborately decorated ones— such as the original Seth Louis Shaw home, built in 1853 by the town's founder—resemble wedding cakes. A stroll past the scrollwork storefronts lining Main Street is a trip to another age; stepping into the Memory Lane Toy Shoppe, for example, is like returning to a happy childhood.

Despite its idyllic setting and other-era atmosphere, Ferndale is a place being pulled in several directions and not knowing which way it wants to go. Old-timers want it to be left alone, but they don't want their town to die. They favor refurbishing the old Victorian homes, since this would preserve Ferndale's uniqueness and wouldn't enlarge the town. Yet it is feared that, if refurbishing is carried too far, the result might be a north coast Disneyland kind of place that would invite mass tourist invasion. Then there is the rumored possibility of the state acquiring Ferndale and turning it into a working Victorian village—a sort of Williamsburg West. This makes everyone shudder.

QUIETTOWN, U.S.A.
Ferndale greets a new morning as mists lift from the flat land of the Eel River Delta. In this pastoral place, one day is pretty much like another, except for a special week in May. Then the annual Art Festival brings creative displays and visitors to Main Street.

NO GITTIN'...JUST SITTIN'
In Ferndale there's no hurry to go anywhere, and not much to do when you get there. The best part of a day can be whiled away sitting on a bench, greeting any neighbors who might happen along.

"Gingerbread Mansion"

"Picket Fence House"

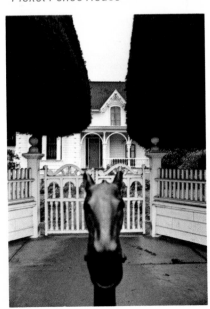

"Gumdrop House"

SMALL TOWN . . . BIG HOUSES
Back in those days when families were big
and stayed in one place for a long time, folks
built good-sized homes and lived in
them for several generations. In Ferndale is
preserved some of the country's most
beautiful old-time architecture.

"Going around the block" is an old Humboldt County expression for taking a leisurely trip through the Mattole River Valley. Bypassing a portion of U.S.101, you'll drive 75 miles or so.

After leaving Ferndale, the route swings up through a natural landscape of oak-dotted hills and grassy meadows, then swoops down in a series of tight hairpin curves toward windy Cape Mendocino, westernmost point of the continental United States. Beyond are Petrolia and Honeydew, the only towns along the way.

Past Honeydew the road executes a series of switchbacks and oxbows as it unwinds into Humboldt Redwoods State Park and then takes a couple of wild curves, as if in defiance of civilization, before joining U.S. 101 north of Weott.

COUNTRY WITH FEW TOWNS

Up hill and down valley twists the unsigned Mattole Road. At one point the route crosses Mattole River near Petrolia (right), where in 1861 California's first oil derricks were raised. The land is open, uncluttered by human habitation, most of it trod only by sheep. "I don't care what the maps show," declared a rancher. "There ain't no more Capetown. You open a gas station there and you'll have a monopoly. You won't have no customers, but you'll have a by-God monopoly."

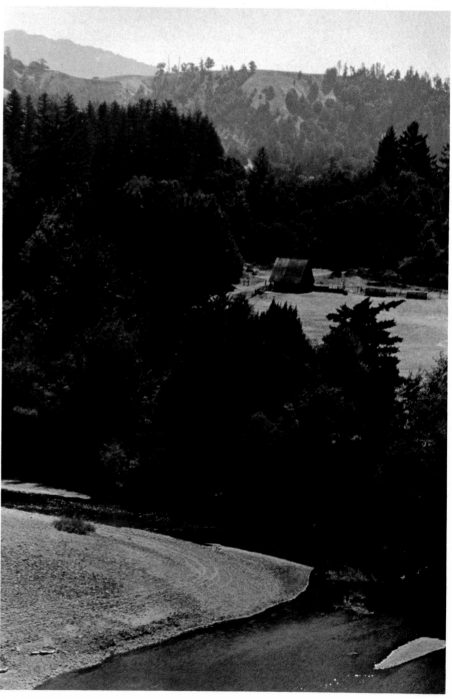

TURN OFF
the highway
to MATTOLE
back country

TOWN WITH FEW HOMES
Though it hasn't many houses, Honeydew boasts a general store, a gas station, a post office, a fire station, and a community hall—all located in the same building. Mattole summers are fiercely hot and winters wet. In 1957-58, 174 inches of rain were recorded.

DETOUR down the Avenue of the GIANTS

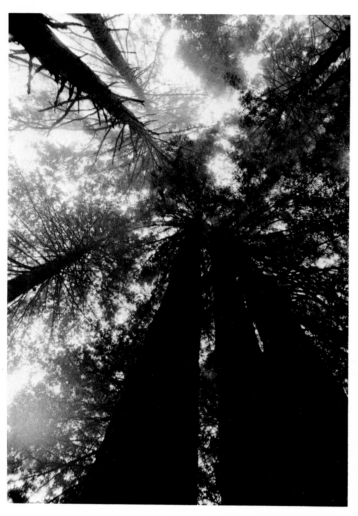

Looking for a less hurried way through a section of the Redwood Empire? Try Avenue of the Giants, a low-speed, scenic route that parallels a busy, sometimes hectic, stretch of U.S. 101, traversing Humboldt Redwoods State Park from Phillipsville on the south to Pepperwood on the north. Crisscrossing the Eel River's south fork, the road meanders along in no great hurry, passing through grove after grove of redwoods, some of them featuring hiking trails, picnic tables, and campgrounds. Along the way are a goodly number of shops selling redwood burls ("Stick them in water, and you'll grow a redwood tree!") and rockhound supplies. There are even a couple of drive-through trees for those who enjoy driving through trees.

BIG-TREE COUNTRY
"In the redwoods you look up, not out,"
goes a saying. In spite of nature's whims and
man's needs, the tenacious redwood
lives on, and in few places is this will to exist
more apparent than at the Immortal Tree,
right. The greater part of the Avenue curves
through second-growth forest that bears
evidence of previous logging: massive
stumps, toppled trunks, traces of skid roads.

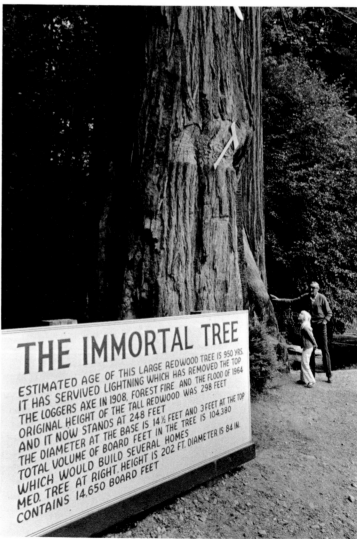

THE IMMORTAL TREE
ESTIMATED AGE OF THIS LARGE REDWOOD TREE IS 950 YRS.
IT HAS SERVIVED LIGHTNING WHICH HAS REMOVED THE TOP
THE LOGGERS AXE IN 1908, FOREST FIRE AND THE FLOOD OF 1964
ORIGINAL HEIGHT OF THE TALL REDWOOD WAS 298 FEET
AND IT NOW STANDS AT 248 FEET
THE DIAMETER AT THE BASE IS 14½ FEET AND 3 FEET AT THE TOP
TOTAL VOLUME OF BOARD FEET IN THE TREE IS 104,380
WHICH WOULD BUILD SEVERAL HOMES
MED. TREE AT RIGHT. HEIGHT IS 202 FT. DIAMETER IS 84 IN.
CONTAINS 14,650 BOARD FEET

GIANT OF THE AVENUE
A MEMORIAL TO THE LOGGERS, WOODSMEN, AND PIONEERS WHO CONQUERED THIS SAVAGE BUT PEACEFUL LAND

To Eureka

Pepperwood

Eel River

Weott

N

Myers Flat

Phillipsville

To Garberville

AVENUE OF THE GIANTS, GIANT OF THE AVENUE
Phillipsville Giant of the Avenue, fashioned by chain saw, looms in front of the Saw Blade Tavern. The popular watering hole is well frequented on a scorching summer's day.

ALL IN A DAY'S WORK
With the touch of a master organist, the edgerman plays his fingers over an electronic console. The controls operate a monstrous, clanking machine that slices lengths of lumber from large slabs. Mill noises are not so fierce as to drown out the shriek of quitting whistle, the signal for everyone to grab his lunchbox and head for home, below.

SCOTIA is one of America's last COMPANY towns

Built by and for employees of Pacific Lumber Company, Scotia is a self-sustaining town with a bank, post office, department store, hotel, barber shop, and—the reason for it all—lumber mill. Of the 1,050 persons who live in Scotia (the population has remained essentially the same since the '20s), virtually every one works for the company, either at the mill, in the woods, or in a service capacity. It is a benign place that provides not only jobs but also homes and security for its residents.

Though proudly independent, Scotia invites visitors to view the log storage pond and take a self-guided tour along the catwalks of Mill B and the factory. Tours start in the former Scotia First National Bank building.

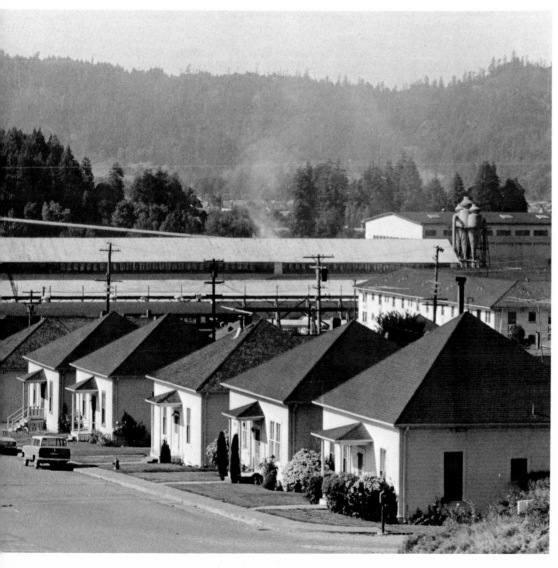

HOME IS WHERE THE HEARTH IS
Most Pacific Lumber employees live in company-built and company-owned houses, paying minimum rent. Maintenance and repairs are done promptly by company plumbers, electricians, or carpenters.

Roaming the KING RANGE— California's lost coast

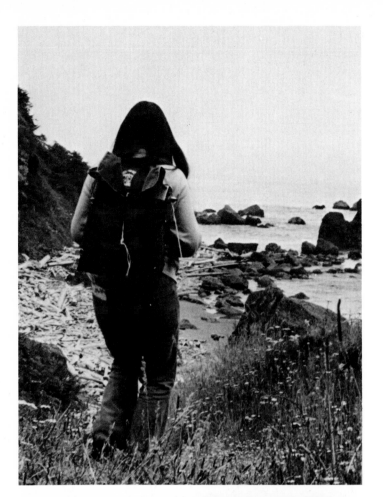

It's one of the state's last pockets of coastal wilderness. It's a ragged, rugged territory of timbered mountains thrusting up 4,000 feet from the Pacific shore, and long stretches of smooth, clean, barely accessible beaches. Some call it the "lost coast"; others call it a wilderness The Bureau of Land Management—which administers its 540,000 acres—designates it a National Conservation Area, the first of its kind in the United States. It's the King Range and it's near Cape Mendocino, some 230 miles north of San Francisco.

The whole place is a kind of pilot model, a multiple-use testing ground for determining if conservation aims, recreational needs, and commercial interests can coexist. According to the BLM, the management program "... provides for a balance of use and protection that will enable the King Range to contribute toward the material needs of the nation while preserving the unique seashore environment." In other words, part of the area is to be kept in its wild state, part is to be used for recreation, and part is to be selectively logged, with revenues being used to expand and consolidate the land holdings.

Though the King Range is not a designated wilderness, no roads mar its natural landscape. The only way to drive there is by taking the Shelter Cove Road from Redway on U.S. 101 to King Range County Road. Situated off the rough county road are developed campgrounds (water, tables, toilets). Primitive forest camps are located along trails heading down the west slope.

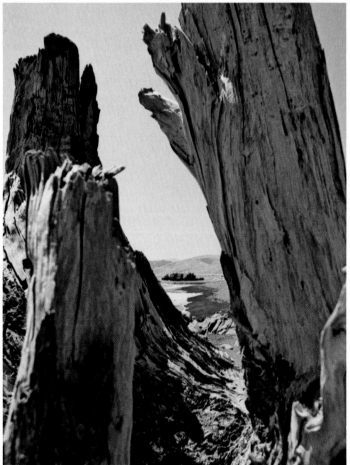

EVERY STEP
A NEW SCENE
Heavily timbered slopes, tangled brushlands, grassy meadows, rocky bluffs, and isolated beaches offer striking variety for the backpacker. Improved campgrounds, with toilets, piped water, are located off King Range County Road on east slope of range.

VIEW FROM THE TOP
One of the least accessible stretches of California coastline, the King Range plunges from a maximum elevation of 4,086 feet to sea level, in some areas almost straight down.

...KING RANGE

SOUTHERN END
OF A RUGGED RANGE

Along with its adjoining mountains, the King Range has isolated a considerable portion of the California coast from the mainstream of north-south activity. Logging flourished in the area until 1930s when reduction of timber caused a retreat of population and nature went back to normal. Today, limited timber cutting is permitted by the Bureau of Land Management.

J.Y. BRYAN

SOMETIMES THERE'S SUN,
SOMETIMES THERE'S NONE
East slopes—where recreation areas are
located—have many sunny days. In summer,
the seaward side of the range may lie
fogbound for weeks, above. Because of its
inaccessibility, the area below—viewed from
Shelter Cove—is referred to as
California's "lost coast."

Mendocino

The Quiet Coast—Its Slumbering

Tranquil and calm is the greater part of the Mendocino-Sonoma coast, as peaceful as the mists that creep over its capes and slip into its coves. To the north the shoreline is indented with sheltered beaches and punctuated by ragged headlands; southward, the face of the land changes to wooded slopes and grassy terraces that drop abruptly to a sea-chewed shore. Quiet though it is, this coastal region receives a goodly number of visitors because of its proximity to San Francisco.

From sleepy Rockport town all the way south to the Russian River—and beyond—State 1 courses like another kind of river, keeping so close to the shore that it hardly disrupts nature's contours. Slipping across steep hillsides and sliding through stands of cypress and eucalyptus, this stream of a highway flows over countryside that has been trodden by Indians, explored by Spaniards, settled by Russians, and emigrated to by New Englanders.

Here is open country, as honest as the people who live on it. Relatively light is the press of population; yet some parts of the region are feeling the pressure of incipient urbanization. Though decrying "the ills of civilization," some residents of the region desire a degree of economic growth. And despite increasing urbanizing influences that manifest themselves in the form of proliferating clusters of hillside homes, they feel there is enough land, enough open space, to accommodate others without their beloved Mendocino country being devoured by overdevelopment.

Country

Days are Numbered

. . . the mist, dispelled from the land, rolled on before the refreshing sea wind, discovering cape after cape, and exhibiting a luxuriant country apparently abounding in wood and rivers.

—Frederick William Beechy

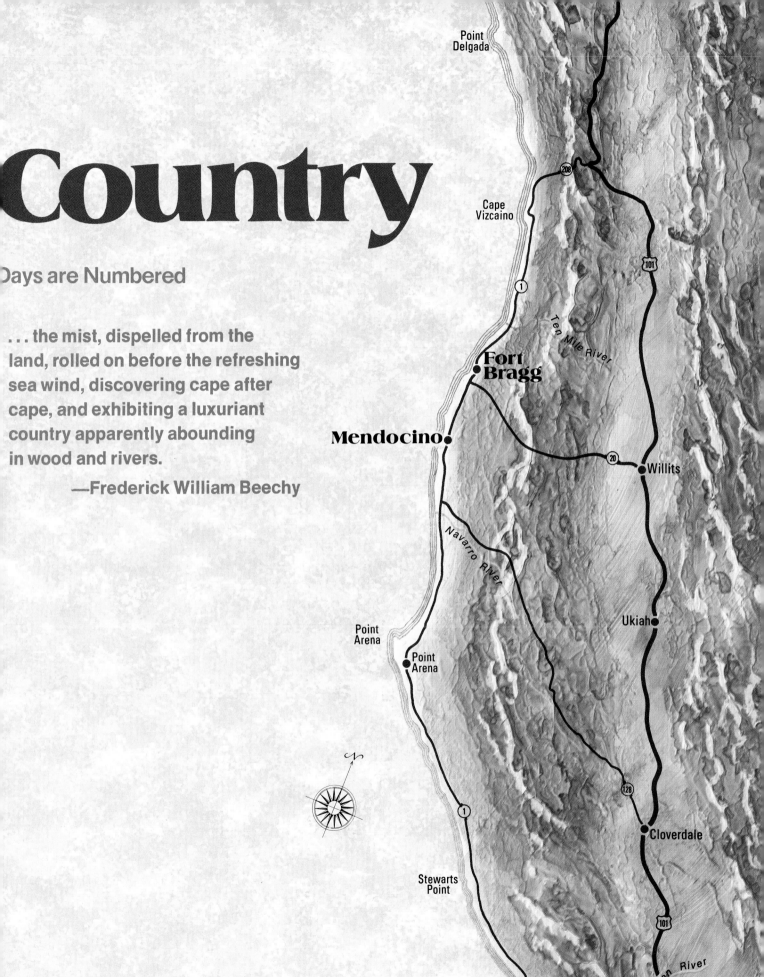

Rockport's a GHOST, Westport ALMOST

Most maps show the first town at the northern end of State 1—the coast highway—to be Rockport. But Rockport is not on the highway. Nor is it a town. State 1 crosses Cotoneva Creek some 20 miles south of Leggett, and that's where Rockport *used* to be. It began as a sawmill in the late 1870s. For 80 years afterward, mills on the site either burned down or shut down, and today only a few shacks remain, occasionally peopled by bands of itinerant free-livers.

A dozen miles farther south—straddling the coast highway—is Westport. In its heyday Westport had a wharf that was a source of local pride because it stretched 400 feet out over the water. The wharf is long gone, and Westport no longer hums with activity but drowses in its own dream of yesterday.

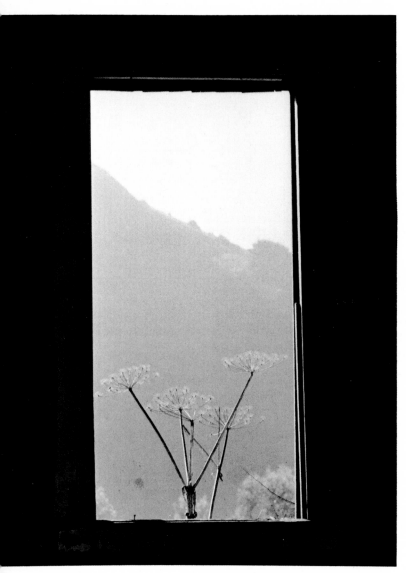

ROCKPORT'S VIEW WITH A ROOM
*Mill shut-downs, frequent fires, and other misfortunes have taken their toll on Rockport. Little remains of the one-time bustling lumber town—located near the south fork of Cotoneva Creek—other than a **couple of dilapidated shacks.***

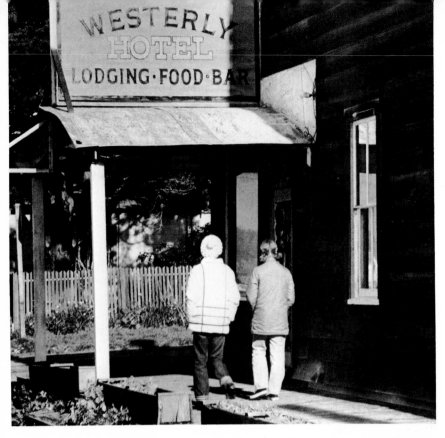

WESTPORT—LIVING ON, MAINLY IN MEMORIES

Gray goats browse the fields, yellow cats snooze the fence tops, and the weather-worn Westerly Hotel sign promises more than it delivers. Usually closed, the aged establishment rests neglected and unloved alongside State 1. At the south end of town rises a neatly painted white home, below. Well maintained, it reflects a cared-for look.

THE WAY WEST... AND EAST

The direction is due east-west, but for a good part of the trip the track doubles back on itself, aiming the engine toward all points of the compass. At Northspur water stop, steamy sighs of Super Skunk's 2-8-2 Mikado locomotive blend with the happy chatter of passengers who scramble aboard the cab for a glimpse of its workings.

Did you ever ride a SKUNK through the REDWOODS?

Comments weren't complimentary, but sentiment has kept the trains running. "You can smell the dang things before you see them," local people used to say of the first gas engines of California Western Railroad Company, as the locomotives huffed and puffed through the woods.

A logging railroad when it began in 1885, the California Western switched to passenger service in 1904, tugging sleeping cars and coaches on the twisting route between Fort Bragg and Willits. Rolling along as dependably as ever and exhuding more merriment than miasma, the line continues to carry both passengers and light freight along the 40-mile right of way owned by Georgia-Pacific lumber company. Self-powered "Skunk" rail cars run the year around; "Super Skunk" steam trains chug and clank during the summer season.

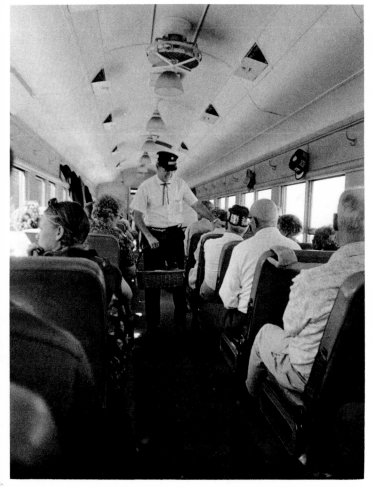

"GET THEM WHILE THEY'RE HOT!"
The snacks aren't really hot, but Skunk's peanut butcher does a landoffice business dispensing them along with generous amounts of joviality, left. At Fort Bragg an imperturbable conductor gathers tickets from eager passengers.

A RAGGED COAST
Jumbled islets and rocky coves make up the
Fort Bragg coastside, a stretch not easily
accessible except by boat. Though the fort
of Bragg is long gone, the town did have
a military detachment, established in 1857
for the purpose of keeping peace
among northern Indians.

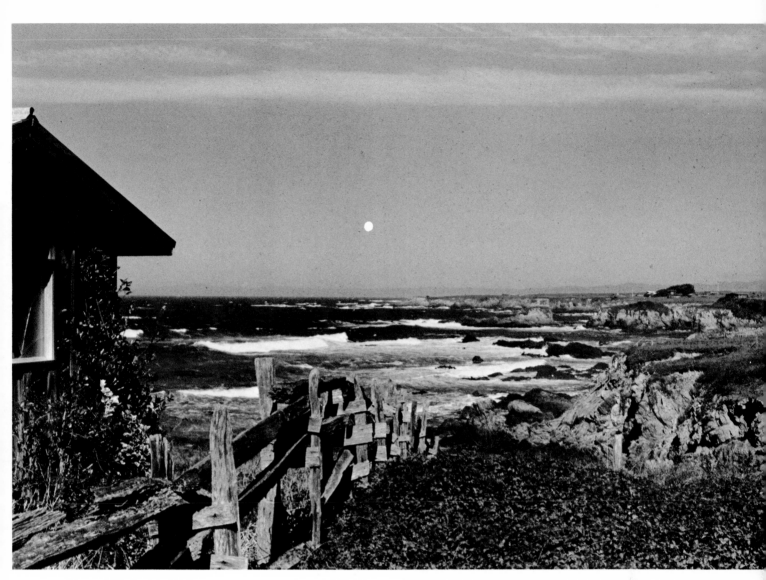

A SHORE THAT
SHARES A DREAM

Around "Cliff House" a tangled wild has been reclaimed to produce a coastal horticultural jewel just south of Fort Bragg. Its creator, Ernest Schoefer, has spent his retirement years turning a wilderness into a seaside garden that is open to the public. "I do it," says Ernest, "because I love nature and I want others to be able to enjoy nature."

As you cross over the Noyo River just south of Fort Bragg, you catch a glimpse to your landward side of what looks to be the model for a Norman Rockwell painting of a Maine fishing village. Take the road at the bridge's north end. It drops down to Noyo Flat, a colorful collection of fish processing plants, bait shops, restaurants, charter boats, and commercial fishing vessels. Stroll along the docks and observe catches of deep-water fish being winched out of holds (the commercials leave at 4 A.M. and return about twelve hours later). Sign on for a sport fishing excursion (they also start early). Watch nets and crab pots being mended. Or just sit on a wooden piling—it doesn't matter whether the sun is shining or whether fog lies on the river—and listen to the wood creakings and gull cryings, letting your senses soak up the spirit of the place.

THE QUIET TIME
Processing plants are silent and docks are practically deserted for most of the day when commercial fishermen are busy at sea. A stay-ashore crew spends the late-afternoon hours repairing crab pots and coiling lines in readiness for the next morning's set.

NOYO is everyone's notion of a fishing VILLAGE

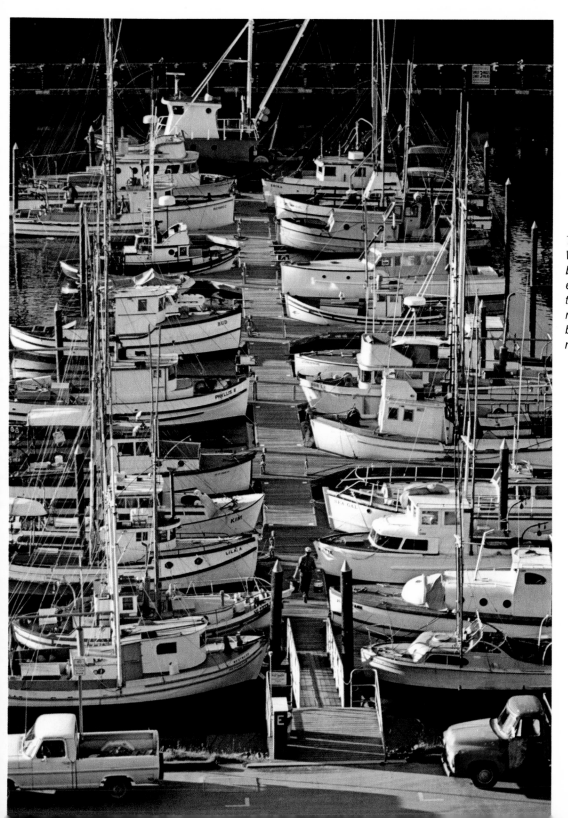

THE CROWDED TIME
When weather outside the breakwater is rough, everyone stays in, and the basin bristles with masts. Too broad to fit a berth, one craft has to moor at far end of dock.

Under the CHUTE, or memories of DOGHOLE days

At the turn of the century, overland travel along the coast was slow and uncertain. To handle shipments of lumber, livestock, and passengers between Northern California and San Francisco—as well as to other world ports—a string of small stations sprouted all along the redwood coast. If a cove was big enough for a dog to turn around in, it was big enough to be pressed into service. Strong tides, heavy winds, and high seas conspired to make the life of a doghole skipper a lively one, and a variety of fantastic contrivances were rigged to get the supplies between ship and shore. Port names such as Hard Scratch, Nip 'n Tuck, and Rough and Ready spoke volumes about the character of the places.

LEISURELY PACE
A pleasant morning in 1916 saw Captain Schuler Mitchell, his family, and friends coolly riding Noyo's trapeze wire to shore from the big schooner Irene. *On a working day, lumber took their place or else was sent streaking down a greased chute to a ship moored under the contraption's end. Chute at right was at Nip n' Tuck.*

QUIET PLACE

From 1861 to 1955, Caspar was a busy shipping port with a wharf, mill, and railroad that ran east for 35 miles. In 1966 much of the town was demolished, following a fire, and today a few homes, a tavern, and the Lighthouse Foursquare Church are about all that remain.

THE DOGHOLE COAST

In the early 1900s, any inside curve in the shore served as a port. Many have vanished without a trace; those shown on the map have survived as tranquil towns.

Without its FENCES the place would have a lot less CHARM

Time has treated them gently. Weather has alternately bleached and stained them the color of the soil from which they rise. On their posts grow lumps of moss. On their rails spread blobs of lichen. Lurching crazily, they stagger over the hills, starting nowhere, stopping nowhere, only *being*. Green vines embrace their solidity; golden grasses support their frailty. They lean with the dignity of old age and topple with a sigh of relief.

Cleone, north of Fort Bragg

Stewart's Point, Sonoma County

Greenwood Road, near Elk

Near Bodega, Sonoma County

Fort Ross, north of Jenner

Valley Ford, east of Bodega Bay

Mendocino town

Mendocino:
The Silent Shore
Saved by the State

Peace and quiet are its chief assets. But as more people go there to enjoy its stillness, the less serene it becomes.

Mendocino's tranquil mien gives little indication of behind-the-scenes turbulence that bubbles up from time to time. No one strolling the silent streets would imagine that in 1854—shortly after its founder, "Honest" Harry Meiggs, took all the money and ran—the mill settlement grew so fast that it almost became the county seat. Mendocino had hotels, saloons, a grand Masonic Hall, a Chinatown. But after the mill closed down, the place fell asleep and snoozed for a long while —until serious artists found the town to their liking and began settling in.

The happy face of the town attracted not only artists and casual visitors but also folks who made up their minds to have a house there. Property values rocketed, new homes popped up like mushrooms after a rain, and residential developments began to appear. It seemed as if the next step might be high-rise condominiums, street lights, and neon signs.

Then the State of California entered the not-so-peaceful-any-more picture. In 1972 the open headland fronting on Mendocino Bay was acquired by the Department of Parks and Recreation with the intent to preserve its natural appearance. The shore was saved, and today a kind of enforced tranquility prevails.

MEMORIES OF MAINE
Shingled roofs and a boxed-in water tower are heritage of early settlers from New England. The ragged shore reminded them of home.

A WALK IN TIME
Some say that the town is too quaint, too contrived, too busy. But when you roam the short streets on a lonely week day, you know that, even with its ever-increasing popularity, Mendocino is all right and will remain that way.

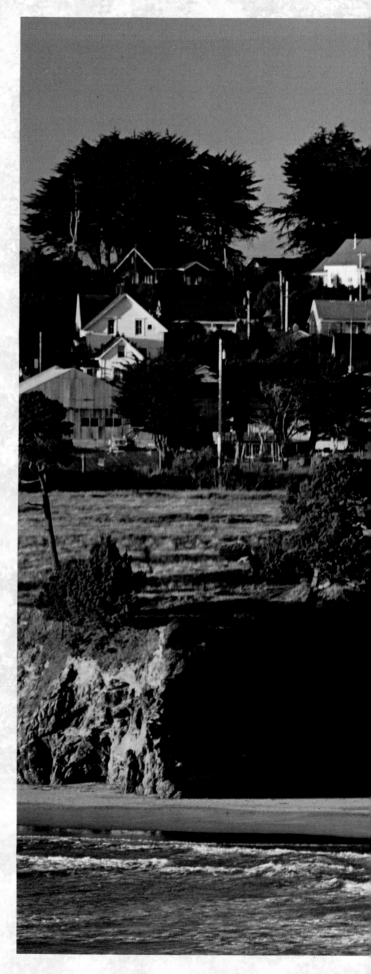

CHANGE COMES SLOW
IN MENDOCINO

"The town presents a beautiful picture as it is approached
from the south on a midsummer's day, with its white
cottages, painted business houses, and modest yet beautiful
places of learning . . . all basking in the sunlight, with
the quiet bay as foreground and the swelling throbbing bosom
of the blue ocean . . . and the evergreen pines and fir
trees." Mendocino today? Yes. And Mendocino almost a
hundred years ago, which was when this
description was written.

Once a quiet COAST, now a stirring SHORE

Known the world over for its equable climate, its scenic wonders, and its beneficent living conditions, the California coast has attracted great numbers of people. Unfortunately, many of them view the shoreline not as a natural resource but as a region of potential development. Public concern over the not-so-gradual transformation of California's shoreline was the prime reason for passage—in 1972—of Proposition 20, an initiative whose purpose is prevention of further coast deterioration while preserving its environment. Perhaps the greatest source of coastline change is the growth of cities. Owing generally to population growth, older, urbanized areas are being more intensively developed, putting a strain on existing roads and recreation areas. Suburban sprawl—the pushing out from population centers—tends to consume vast natural resources. Second-home development, far from centers of trade and employment, creates thousands of pockets of private property that deny access to the shoreline except to a select few.

The problem of making the maximum amount of coastline readily available to the maximum number of people has no pat answers. However, some proposals aimed at balancing human needs against preservation of natural resources are being considered.

One possibility is establishing a continuous band for public use along the coastline. Another is opening coastal portions of public lands to the public. Others include limiting developments that block coastal access or views; concentrating development in existing urban areas, while setting up expansion boundaries; reducing the number of lots in coastal subdivisions; and restoring degraded coastal resources.

HARD-TO-REACH SHORE
Though California's shoreline is in the public domain, reaching it can sometimes be a puzzle. By law, owners of adjoining property may not prevent beach use, but they can make getting to the water difficult.

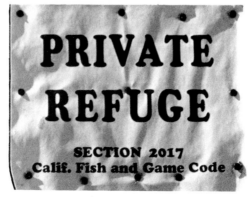

The hand of man has lightly touched this section of
Mendocino coast. The weathered fence is more a token
boundary than a barrier. The slender road snakes
inconspicuously along the shore. Only the tree-ragged
hillsides reflect a marked change in the natural landscape.
They are a memento of a time when thick forest
crowded down the slopes almost to the water's edge.

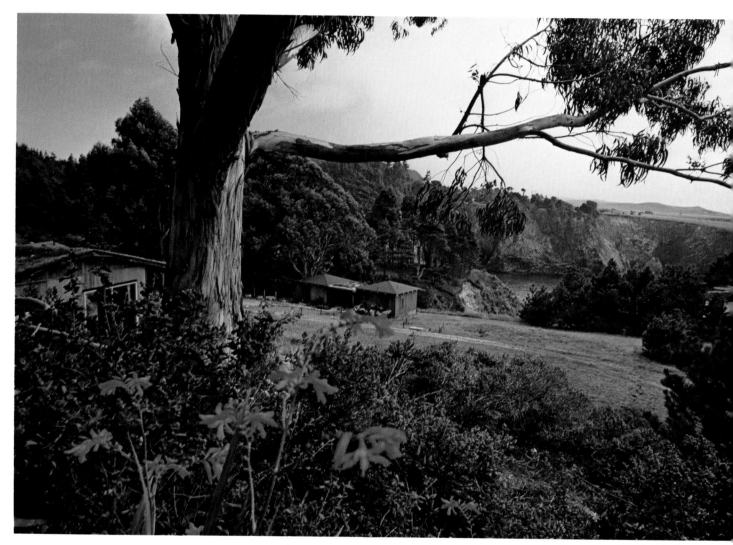

A BIT OF THE PAST, *Scalloped coves, open meadows, and cottages tucked into*
INCLUDING *the landscape are part of the experience at Heritage*
OLD-FASHIONED HOSPITALITY *House, located at Little River. In the past a farm, a shipping point, a smuggling base, and a hideout for gangster "Baby Face" Nelson, the area is now a placid retreat for those yearning to escape the ferment of city life.*

The old INNS: creature comforts with a touch of YESTERDAY

George Washington never slept in any of them, but that hardly takes away from their delightfulness. Spotted along a 20-mile stretch of the coast highway from Mendocino south are a handful of country inns, some perching on bluffs overlooking the ocean, others snuggled into the foothills on the land side of the road, a few peeking out of tree-thick coves opening onto the sea.

Several of the fine, old structures date back to the mid-1800s. One was built as an executive mansion for a lumber company; one was a grand, Maine-style mansion; a few began as humble farmhouses. Whatever their origin may be, their cozy fireplaces, comfortable rooms, and fine food create a warm atmosphere that cannot be readily found in a regular hotel or motel.

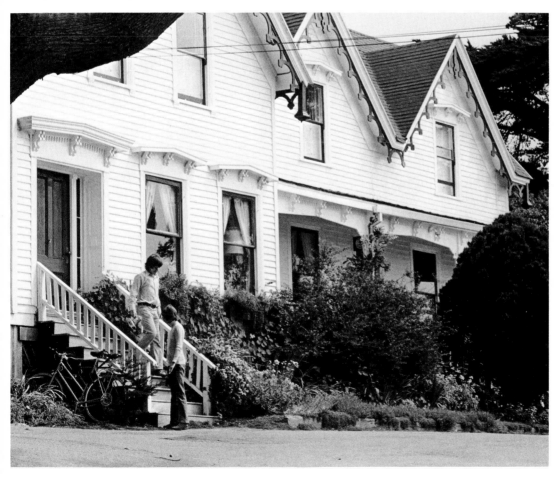

A BIT OF OLD . . . AND NEW
Little River Inn features early California-style rooms with a view of the Pacific. There are also contemporary accommodations, cottage units, and a nine-hole golf course.

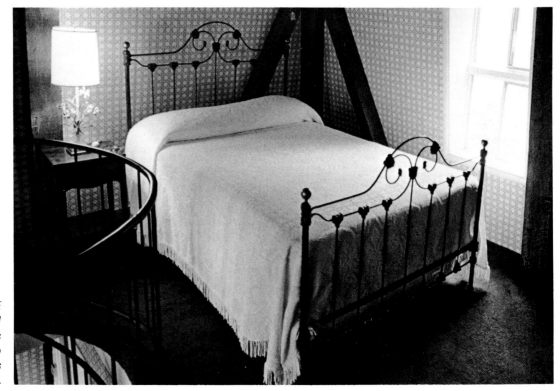

OUTSIDE AND INNSIDE
Scrawny wooden gull maintains vigil outside his namesake in Mendocino town. At right, cozy quarters in a cozy hostel.

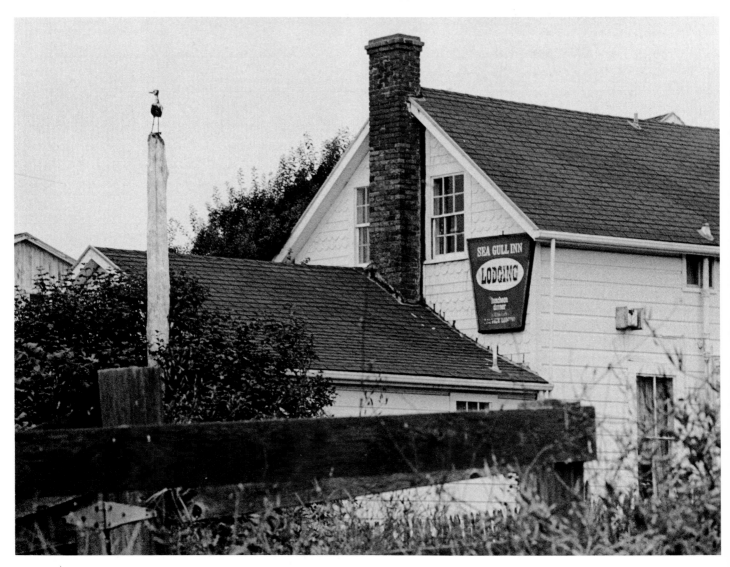

"It was two days to San Francisco by stage, one by steamer..."

Following in a line of ancestors who came to California from Maine in the 1850s, L.D. Dennen —owner and gracious host of the Heritage House—has been witness to many changes in the Mendocino coast.

"When I was just a kid, it was two days to San Francisco by stage, one by steamer in the winter time. To go anywhere we had to ride four-horse stagecoaches—just like you see in the late, late movies.

"When we went to San Francisco, we first had to ride to Plantation—it's up above Sea Ranch —and there we stayed overnight in the hotel. The next day we'd catch a fresh, four-horse stage into Cazadero or Duncan Mills. There we transferred to the caboose of a lumber train and rode as far as Santa Rosa. From Santa Rosa we took what is now the Northwestern Pacific into Sausalito, then boarded the ferry boat for San Francisco.

"All that took two days. So when people come up to me now and say, 'Goodness, it took us three hours to drive here,' I have to chuckle. . . .

"Weather permitting, we sometimes changed our route by taking the Sea Foam, a little steam schooner that ran along the coast. These schooners got into port only in good weather. When it was foul, they passed us by. But when one made it, we'd get aboard about four in the afternoon, and if there weren't any bad delays, we'd be in San Francisco the next morning. It was a nice alternative. Even though some people didn't take to a sea voyage, it was sometimes the better way. . . .

"I don't remember there being a single stretch of paved road in all of the county when I was very young. My grandfather never was able to go to his monthly meeting in Ukiah as a Mendocino County supervisor without having to ride on horseback, because most of the roads—if you want to call them that—weren't good enough to allow travel any other way. . . .

"There aren't many shipwrecks along this coast any more because of radar and other kinds of sophisticated navigation. Nothing on the scale of when I was a youngster.

"We'd hear the distress signal at night, and everybody in the whole community would jump out of bed and rush to get to wherever the boat might be in trouble to see if they could help.

"My mother used to tell about when she lived in Manchester. There are long miles of beach there at Manchester, which is now a state park. The people would go out and build great fires when a ship ran aground. The ship would be pounding and smashing in the dark and the heavy seas, and some of the men would jump overboard and try to swim toward the light of the fire. Some made it, but many didn't. The loss of life was fearful. . . .

"However rugged this area may seem, the people around here were—and are—pretty civilized. Oh, plenty of tough ones came here, but the rougher elements all ended up in the Mother Lode. The ones that stayed around the coast weren't looking for adventure, like some of the others. They were looking for a new frontier—a place where they could settle down and have a new kind of life and raise a family and work hard for their homes."

The RUSSIANS aren't coming...they've already been here

Under the flag of the Russian-American Company (a trade monopoly), Russian frontiersmen in search of seal and otter furs set up outposts in the Aleutians, Alaska, and—in 1812—California. The colony of Ross (an old form of the word *Rosiia,* "Russia" had a fort with a stout wall, or stockade, over a dozen cannon, a commandant's residence, warehouses, and a chapel.

Rebuilt, restored, and protected as a State Historic Park, time-mellowed Fort Ross is located on State 1, some 11 miles north from Jenner. Ships once anchored in the cove below the fort, and kayaks were dried on the rocks above the beach. By half-closing your eyes, you can almost see sailing ships swinging at their anchor lines, skiffs putting out to them with supplies and otter hides, and men carrying loads to and from the shore. The illusion is complete if you touch the heavy mooring chain secured in the ground a short way west of the fort.

UNDER THE DOUBLE EAGLE
Spain occupied most of the lands around the Russian settlement and considered the coast to be its own property by right of first discovery. Russian occupation was regarded as illegal. However, because the Spaniards decided that the stout palisades and blockhouses were impregnable, they never tested the defenses.

Wooden pins lock mortised truss and sills into main posts.

Top truss and sills are locked into main posts spaced about 12 feet apart, extending about 6 feet into ground.

Top truss

Sill

Main post

Punchion slab

Main post

Tops of punchion slabs are held in place by horizontal key locked to upper sill.

Sill

Punchion slabs extend about 4 feet below surface and are mortised into lower sills.

HOW A STOCKADE WAS MADE
Falling substantial timbers in surrounding forests, the Russians built their fort walls high and heavy to withstand expected Indian attacks. But local Indians welcomed the settlement as a safeguard against the less-welcome Spaniards.

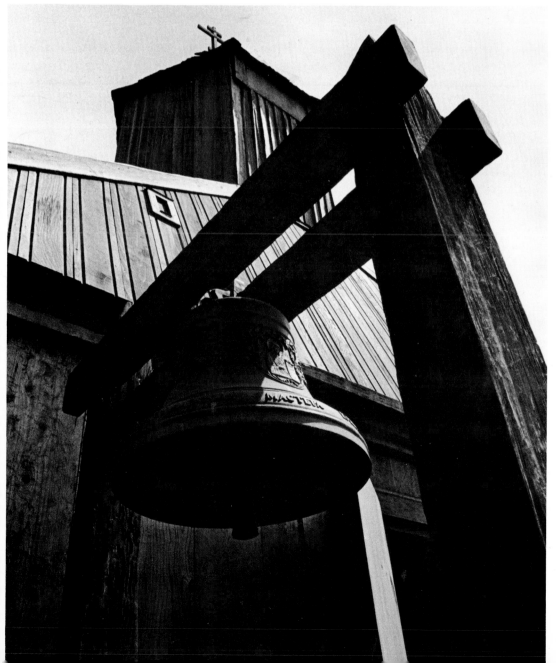

AN OFT-RESTORED CHAPEL
The first chapel was restored in 1917 and again 40 years later, original timbers being retained wherever possible. In 1970 the chapel burned to the ground. Reconstruction, completed in 1974, included a new casting of the lost bell.

And now at last, not even STANDING

Evergreen Cemetery, Point Arena

The Elk Cemetery

The hilltop, Mendocino town

Seafarers' monument, Elk

The names are Irish, Italian, Scandinavian, Portuguese. The origins are Norway, Nova Scotia, the Azores, Maine, Wales. Not at all morbid or depressing, the north coast cemeteries are gentle places washed by the clean wind from the sea. The lichen-spotted headstones are plain, their inscriptions simple. Few speak of a life hereafter, for the north coast people were a sturdy folk who dealt in the present. Here is how one is remembered:

"Always a riddle,
"Never critical, never demanding,
"Never commanding,
"And now, at long last, not even standing."

Odd Fellows' Cemetery, Point Arena

Headstones, Little River

Evergreen Cemetery, Point Arena

AT THE MOUTH AND
A LITTLE WAY BACK
Surf rolls and tumbles in constant agitation where it meets outflow of Russian River at Jenner. Four miles inland, wildflower brilliance almost overpowers the mellowed barn-red color of Duncan Mills store-and-post office.

Side ROAD up the rolling Russian RIVER

Extending for hundreds of yards into the Pacific below Jenner is a turbulent, sometimes silt-brown expanse of water that marks the end (or beginning, depending on how one looks at things) of the Russian River.

Running low and clear during the summer, the river flows faster—and higher—when winter rains swell it. The river bank road (State 116) twists and turns with almost every bend of the water course, passing through quiet redwood groves and often-raucous resort areas. Hordes of summer visitors know the 12-mile cluster of watering places centered on Guerneville, and many fishermen are familiar with the river's riffles, ponds, and holes.

"REACH FOR THE SKY AND KEEP 'EM HIGH"
Pint-sized showdown on porch of general store is Villa Grande's measure of excitement for the week. (Gas pump prices are a carryover from a more carefree day.) The tiny settlement, north of Monte Rio off Moscow Road, is half-hidden by trees. River road, shown on map above, is sometimes inundated by winter flooding.

Golden Gate

 The Scenic Shore—Living i

Above and below San Francisco Bay, the timeless sea cuts into soft coastal rocks, sculpting a shoreline of sandy beaches interspersed with low cliffs. Knifing north from the Golden Gate, that great crack in the earth known as the San Andreas Fault has opened a long, sunken valley near the northern boundary of Marin County—Tomales Bay. On the bay's east side, the land slopes gradually, making fine grazing grounds for sheep and cattle whose time is devoted to cropping the sweet hillside grasses. On the opposite shore, the land is rocky, irregular, and dotted with cottages.

Other geologic processes have built high bluffs and ridges overlooking the broad break in the coast known as the Golden Gate. For generations man has armed them to guard San Francisco Bay from other-than-natural forces. One of the few advantages of the perfection of the intercontinental missile was the elimination of a need to maintain a fortified coastline, and the gun embankments and bunkers of the Marin and San Francisco coasts have now become the nucleus of a large, multi-use recreational zone—the Golden Gate National Recreation Area.

In San Francisco—and for several miles southward—the tumbled dunes that once made up the coastline were long ago covered over with homes and highway, leaving but a narrow strip of shore. Much of the once-fertile land approaching Half Moon Bay is yielding to burgeoning development, but below that town agricultural lands are yet prominent.

Coast

Harmony with the Sea

Lo! here we sit mid the sun-down seas
And the white sierras. The swift,
    sweet breeze
Is about us here; and the sky
    so fair
Is bending above in its azaline hue. . . .
                        —Joaquin Miller

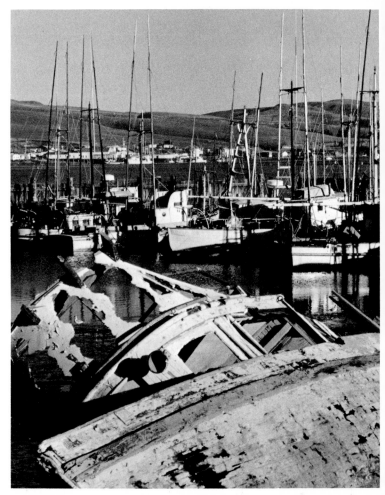

DOWN TO
THE BARE BONES

Stove-in hulls almost outnumber sound ones in Bodega Lagoon. At the north end, high and dry alongside Bay Flat Road, there's even an ancient ferry boat. In spite of the protection offered by Bodega Head and by a long, manmade breakwater, winter storms blast across the bay, whipping its waters into a fury, and beating against houses fronting on the water, below.

BODEGA BAY– beached boats and mud GRUBBERS

Honoring two towns, a bay, and a headland––all in the southwest corner of Sonoma County—the greatly abbreviated name of Spanish explorer Juan Francisco de la Bodega y Cuadra gives coastside explorers a few moments pause. Just what—and where—is Bodega?

Surrounded by pasture land, Bodega village rests in a valley at the intersection of Salmon Creek and the Bodega highway, 4 miles inland from the bay of the same name. At the bay's north end, a broad peninsula (Bodega Head, once slated to be a nuclear power plant site) hooks out from the shore, protecting the lagoon behind it and the town at the lagoon's edge—the town of Bodega Bay.

Along this shore, the greatest activity centers in and around the lagoon. When the tide is out and mudflats are muddiest, the inner harbor is a favored digging ground for clammers. Commercial fishing boats crowd the town docks, and charters work into the bay and out to sea.

DOWN-TO-EARTH DIGGING
Bay's mud flats attract a strange but dedicated type of hunter: the gaper or horseneck clam digger. When he spots a small hole in the mud or a squirt of water (a sure sign of mollusk activity), he pushes a tin cylinder into the ooze. If shoveling out the muck doesn't turn up a clam, he throws himself totally into his work, scrabbling deep with bare hands. Three feet is the practical limit of the metal tubes, but "sometimes the critters feel like they're thirty feet down."

Leaning barns that once were spick-and-span but whose only traces of care are faded tracks of red paint . . . broken-down harrows, hay forks, and tractors that clattered through the fields but whose silent sides are rusting to the color of coffee . . . sagging chicken coops and pig houses that housed battalions of cackling, grunting creatures but whose only sound is the keening of the wind between the wall boards . . . picket fences that stood tall and tight but whose gaps look like toothless smiles . . . one-lane roads that knew the clip-clop of horses' hooves and the crunch of carriage wheels but whose track disappears into the deep shade of weeds.

MELLOW MEMENTOS
Altered by the alchemy of salt air and time,
well-used pieces of agricultural
equipment slowly return to the earth.

Touches of
YESTERDAY
in the coastal
QUIET COUNTRY

RICHARD GROSS

PERIOD OF
PASTORAL MAGIC   Late afternoon sun warms the woolly backs of sheep browsing
a closely cropped hillside. Haze softens the shoreline,
transforming a cluster of rocky islets into ghostly forms.

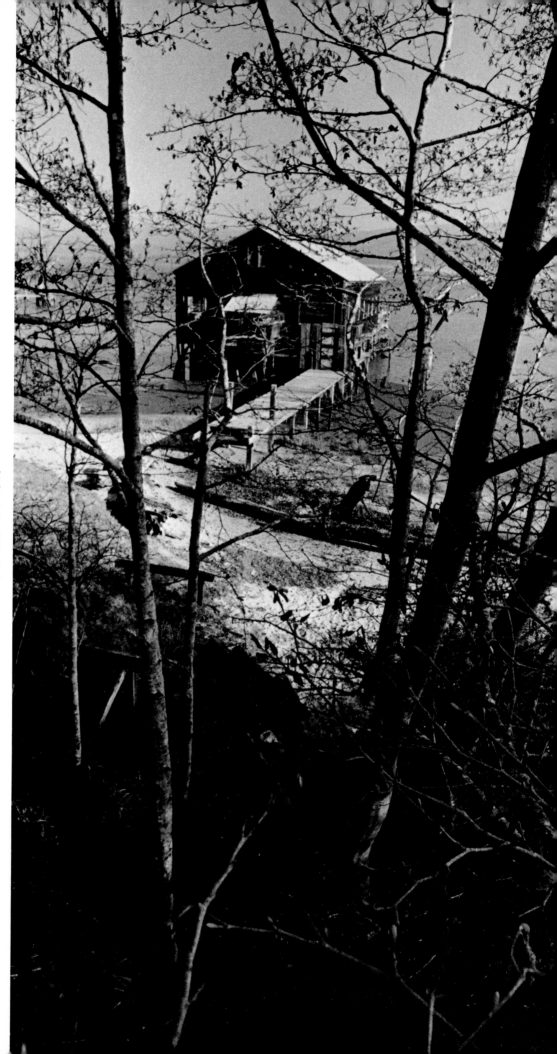

SCREENWORK
AGAINST THE SKY
Like a crackle glaze on pottery, winter-stripped alder branches etch a webbing against sky and bay, framing a weary boathouse whose wharf ends like a gasp.

The venerable BOATHOUSES of Tomales Bay

Tomales Bay once was a handy shelter for schooners serving the farms and dairy ranches out on Point Reyes. In the late 1800s, acres of bay front were subdivided, and the place was ballyhooed as an idyllic resort area, a sailboater's radiant shore. Weekenders from San Francisco used to row on the bay or cruise its waters in launches. During prohibition, rumrunners plied its waters by night, making good use of any available wharf, dock, or boathouse.

Things have quieted considerably around Tomales Bay, and its boathouses are about the only remnants of the "good" old days. Some are sorry heaps of soggy planks while others waver tenuously on worm-eaten pilings. A couple have been metamorphosed into cozy homes.

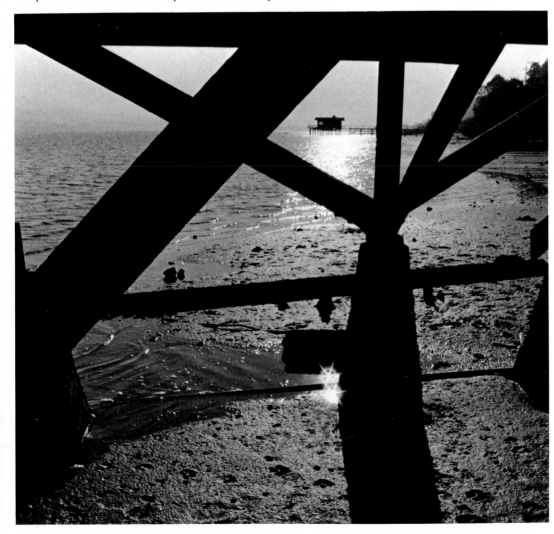

TRACERY ON THE TIDAL FLATS
Bird tracks, dog prints, shellfish siphons, and mysterious craters pattern the jellylike mud under one ancient structure. Concrete pilings support not only wooden underpinnings but barnacles, limpets, and other forms of intertidal life.

...BOATHOUSES

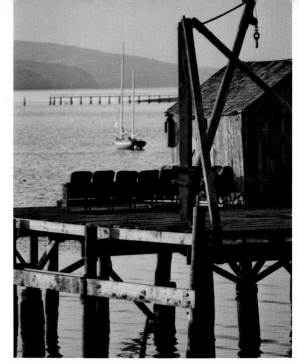

AS PRACTICAL AS IT IS POETIC
A row of resurrected theater chairs (right) handles part of Saturday night overflow from Marshall tavern and restaurant and makes a fine place for watching the sun set. On the other side of Tomales Bay (below), not far from Inverness, a spidery walkway connects with boathouse supported on toothpick legs.

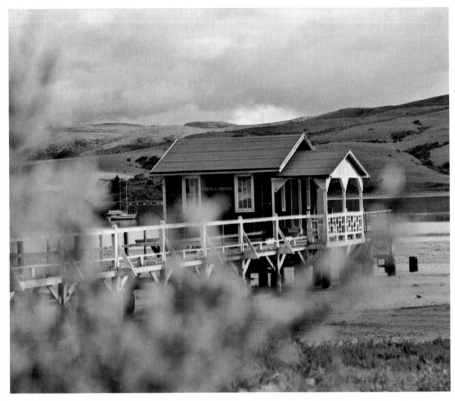

A WALK OVER WATER

When tide is at flood, you can reach a boathouse easily by skiff, but at ebb the most practical way of crossing over the mudflats is to walk above them. Cheerfully painted "Castellammare", left, is a private residence.

BIVALVES BY THE BUSHEL

Johnson Oyster Company owner and his assistant pitch a bargeload of Drake's Bay Oysters onto a conveyor, which carries them into a shoreside building for shucking by hand. Some growers cultivate oysters on mud bottoms, but Charlie Johnson prefers the hanging cult (short for cultures). Oyster seedlings attach to strings of empty shells suspended from a platform, where they mature free from natural enemies—the crab, stingray, and starfish.

Oyster strings

Shallow water

Bottom

These BEDS are wet and full of OYSTERS

Virtually any shore in North America is potential oyster country, but in only a few areas are the tasty bivalves grown in commercial quantities. Thriving in the cool north as well as in the tepid tropics, these communal creatures dwell in shallows where tidal changes remove suffocating sediment and bring them food. Like most shellfish, oysters filter algae and other nutrients out of the water that bathes them.

Because cultivated bivalve beds can produce enormous quantities of edible protein material, oyster and mussel growing is an important part of aquaculture —the farming of food crops in the sea.

Pacific oystering is conducted on public ocean bottom lands that are allotted specifically for oyster culture. California's chief commercial beds are in Humboldt Bay, Tomales Bay, Drake's Estero, and Morro Bay. Pity the poor California oyster, whose sex life is stymied by cold water. It can grow, but since it is unable to properly spawn (a process in which one female can release as many as a hundred million eggs), oyster beds are planted with seedlings shipped from Japan, British Columbia, or Washington.

Two philosophies of oyster culture prevail. One involves spreading the seedlings in beds on the bottom of estuaries. There the oysters are left to grow for about three years and are then harvested by men who slog out to them at low tide. The other method is planting seedlings on empty shells strung on wires that hang in the water. This system keeps the growing oysters off the bottom, away from predators, and allows them to utilize the entire water column for food.

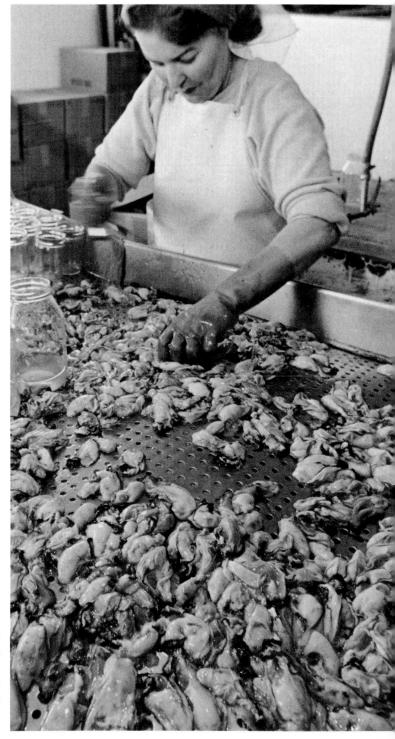

A FOOD FOR ALL SEASONS
Immediately after being shucked, oysters are rinsed with cold water, hand-sorted for size, and packed. Oyster lovers prize the delicate texture and fine flavor of Drake's Bay Ostrea Gigas. Their high quality is due, in part, to the unspoiled waters in which they grow.

Point Reyes:
Primitive Beauty Untouched
by the Hand of Man

It's more than a recreation spot. This island in time increases man's understanding of the past and causes him to think about his future direction.

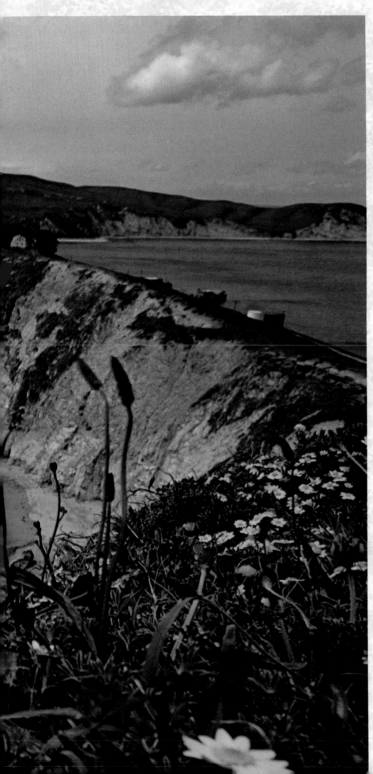

The story of Point Reyes is a tranquil story of nature. The story of Point Reyes is also a tempestuous story of man—of his exploration, his exploitation, his conservation.

Coast Miwok Indians were the first known inhabitants of the quiet peninsula. In wonderment they gazed on the ships of Drake, Cermeno, and Vizcaino. It was Vizcaino who gave a name to the land, calling it Puerto de los Reyes, after the Sacred Day of the Three Kings. When California's Mexican governors handed out great chunks in land grants in the 19th century, thousands of acres of Point Reyes became cattle ranches.

The mid-1950s were the most turbulent, most critical period for the peninsula. Real estate developers began staking out homesites; loggers started tearing into the redwoods; oil exploration raised the ghost of derricks and drilling platforms. Spurred by conservationists, the National Park Service moved into action, working at a feverish pace matched only by that of the bulldozers already slicing into the earth. Public pleas were made, petitions circulated, bills fought through. Finally the storm was over: Point Reyes was saved from development.

In 1966 Point Reyes National Seashore was dedicated. Turning the Sierra Club's "island in time" phrase, Secretary of the Interior Stewart Udall called Point Reyes ". . . an island in the nick of time."

ISLAND IN TIME
This is the very point of Point Reyes, viewed from Chimney Rock at the upper end of Drakes Bay. To the right of this narrow spine of land is Drake's Beach. Though attached to the California mainland, the Point Reyes Peninsula is knifed by the 1906 Rift of the San Andreas Fault, and many geologists believe it will eventually become an island.

IS THIS THE FAIRE AND GOODE BAYE?

In 1597 Sir Francis Drake brought his ocean-weary Golden Hinde somewhere into a California anchorage. Early writings referring to a "... faire and goode baye ... white bancks and cliffes ..." lead many historians to believe that what is now called Drake's Bay was where the ship was careened for repairs. For them the clincher came in the 1930s with the discovery of a brass plate bearing Drake's name.

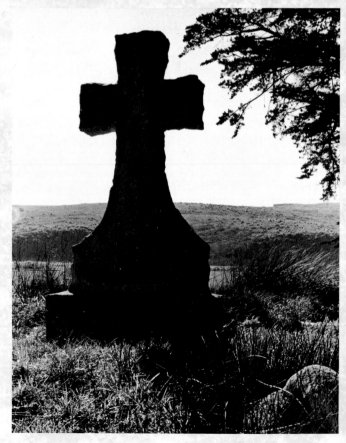

NO SHADOW OF DOUBT
Granite cross at Drake's Bay, erected by Sir Francis Drake Association of California, is unequivocally "In commemoration of the landing of Francis Drake ... on these shores."

HERE'S LOOKING AT YOU
White-faced Hereford and Holstein cattle graze some
sections of pasture still owned by long-time tenant ranchers.
As the National Park Service acquires such lands, fences and
barns are removed, gradually returning
the peninsula to its primitive state.

The WEATHERED western EDGE of California

ON A GOOD DAY...
During months of October, November, December—and between winter storms—California's coast experiences some of its most brilliant weather. Fleecy clouds are not often formed along the shore but build up several miles inland.

Fog, rain, wind, storm. Most of California's weather comes from the west. Cold air slides down from the Aleutians; warm air blows up from the south Pacific. Both are twisted by the earth's rotation to a westerly direction, and the first part of the state to feel climatic change is its seaward side. The coast never becomes as hot or cold as regions several miles to the east because water heats or cools more slowly than land. This is also the reason why seasonal changes along the coast don't follow a "normal" pattern—why summer in San Francisco lags behind summer in Sacramento.

ROY MURPHY

...ON A BAD DAY

When the sky blackens and ominous clouds pile up in the west, dirty weather is on the way. The dark haze between water and cloud layer is an area of heavy rain squalls at sea.

WET IN THE WEST, DRY IN THE EAST

In winter months, warm, moist air blows off the Pacific and is deflected up Coast Ranges, losing heat in its climb. Moisture falls as cold rain on westward side of the mountains. By the time air reaches the mountain tops, most of its water has been wrung out, and it slides down the eastern slopes, growing warmer and absorbing water along the way.

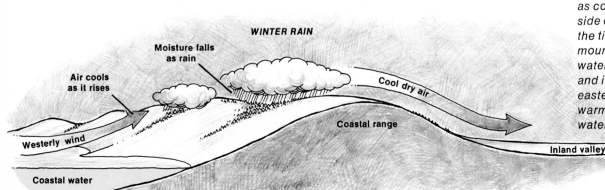

WINTER RAIN

Moisture falls as rain

Air cools as it rises

Cool dry air

Coastal range

Westerly wind

Inland valley

Coastal water

99

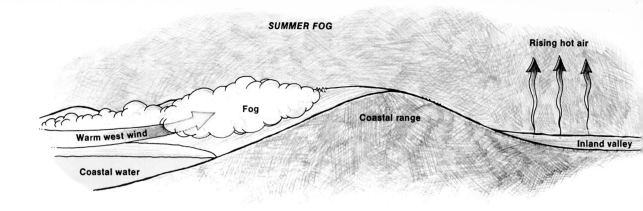

SUMMER FOG

Rising hot air

Fog

Coastal range

Warm west wind

Inland valley

Coastal water

*CALIFORNIA FOG COMES,
BUT NOT ON LITTLE CAT FEET*
*Disconcerting to first-time visitors is California's summertime
coastal fog. Even inland dwellers, heading for seaside sun,
often find their favorite beach completely socked in. There's
no out-guessing coastal fog. A few hundred feet in any
direction—including straight up—may reveal blue skies.*

WEATHER IN A WORD—FOG!
During summer, damp air blows off the ocean toward land. About twenty miles away from the coast, it meets a band of cold water—the California Current—and condenses as fog. Rising hot air inland pulls fog against the Coastal Range. "When it's foggy on the coast," the saying goes, "it's hot in the valley."

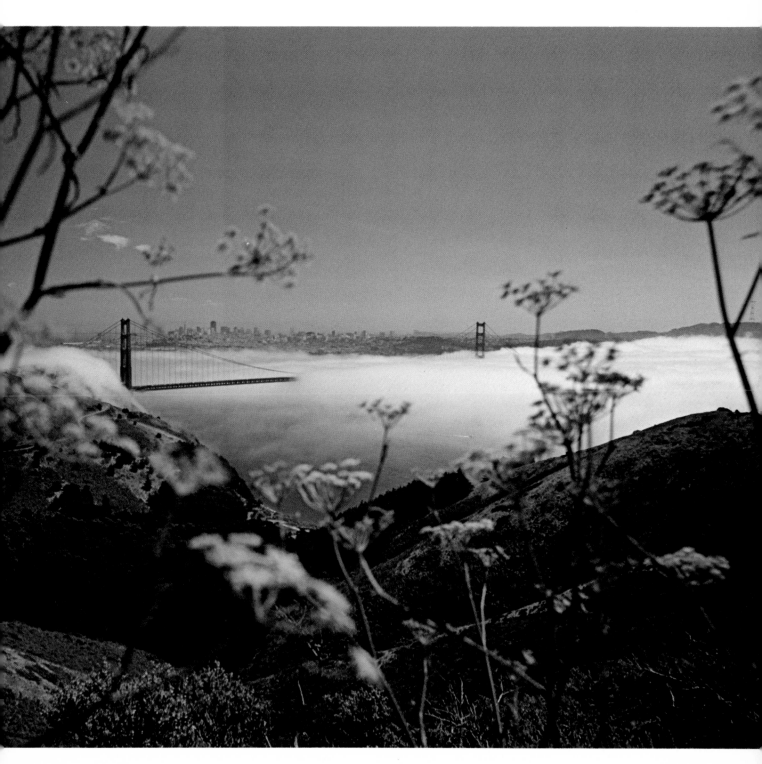

SAILERS and steamers – a gallery of coastal CRUISERS

ABNER COBURN, *a down-easter built in Maine for the California grain trade.*

From Europe, South America, the Orient, Australia, and the east coast of the United States they sailed for California. Converging on San Francisco, the clippers and schooners and barks brought adventurous men and women who were eager to experience the golden land. Some of the vessels carried people; others were laden with cargos of food, tools, and trade goods. After unloading, many ships left, never to return. Some became part of a fleet that connected California with the rest of the world. A few stayed on, trafficking up and down the coast to tie together remote settlements.

COLORADO, *one of Pacific Mail's side-wheel steamers that transported United States mail to China and Japan.*

FORESTS OF MASTS
San Francisco's heyday as a port came during Gold Rush days. In 1850 the waterfront was jammed with vessels that had beat their way up and down the coast from all parts of the world, bearing cargos of gold seekers and supplies. Some of the ships sailed on to other ports; many were abandoned at their moorings.

LILY, *a fore-and-aft rigged lumber schooner built to sail close to California's coast.*

FLYING CLOUD, *a passenger-carrying clipper that ran from Boston to San Francisco in 89 days.*

BOWHEAD, *a steam whaling bark—her rigging interwoven with drying whalebone—that ran to Arctic Seas.*

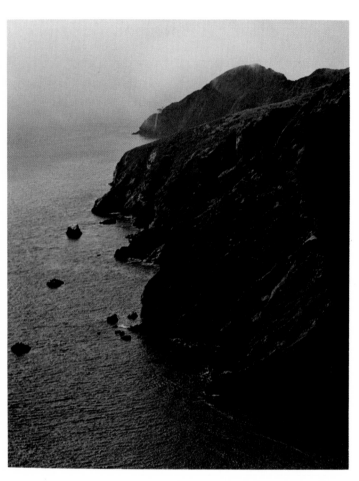

Its northern boundary is the town of Olema, situated at the edge of Point Reyes National Seashore; its southern extremity is Fort Funston, at the foot of San Francisco County. Its 34,000 acres of land and water take in undeveloped coast, state and county parks, military reservations, museums, islands, and privately owned properties that are gradually being acquired for public use. Its setting of rugged, open land, urban park areas, and ocean front makes Golden Gate National Recreation Area unlike any other place in the world.

Much of the Marin headlands at the north end of Golden Gate Bridge was formerly military property. Now the abandoned gun batteries and lonely walls—some of them dating to the Civil War—are open for exploration. Excursions to Alcatraz Island (a maximum security federal penitentiary from 1934 until 1963) and Angel Island (a place of wooded slopes, steep hiking trails, and old army barracks) are adventures in themselves. Among other fortifications that offer an opportunity to relate the history of coastal defense from 1776 are Fort Point, the Presidio, and Fort Mason (headquarters for the recreation area). South of Golden Gate is heavily used urban parkland: Aquatic Park and Pier, Gashouse Cove, Marina Green, Lincoln Park, and Ocean Beach.

The Golden Gate Recreation Area is a place with tremendous use potential. As public awareness of the area increases, more and more people will begin to experience this unique recreational resource.

GOLDEN GATE'S NORTHERN EDGE
Rugged Marin headlands plunge almost straight down to meet waters flowing in and out of San Francisco Bay. Until 1974, most inland area was a vast military reservation, closed to the public.

JUST INSIDE THE GATE
Anglers do their thing at Fort Baker, near the northeast end of Golden Gate Bridge, as a fishing boat chugs along, homeward bound.

Room to RAMBLE– exploring the Golden Gate RECREATION area

PETER FRONK

*GOLDEN GATE PROMENADE—
LONG-FORGOTTEN VIEWS OF THE CITY*

Vistas seldom seen by most San Franciscans open along the shore from Aquatic Park, at the foot of Van Ness Avenue, to Fort Point, huddled under the south end of Golden Gate Bridge. Even on a chilly, windy day, it's a delightful stroll.

THE SCENE OUT TO SEA
From Muir Beach Lookout the view is . . .
varying. At times it can be crystal clear; then
again, it may be fuzzed over with fog, drifting
and shifting and occasionally offering a
quick glimpse of the shore far below.

SOMETIMES A SLOWER STEP...
Sunning his back, an old-timer sits for quiet minutes, perhaps remembering busier yesterdays. Since the gradual decline of shipping from many Pacific ports, time has been gentle with some parts of San Francisco's waterfront, harsh with others.

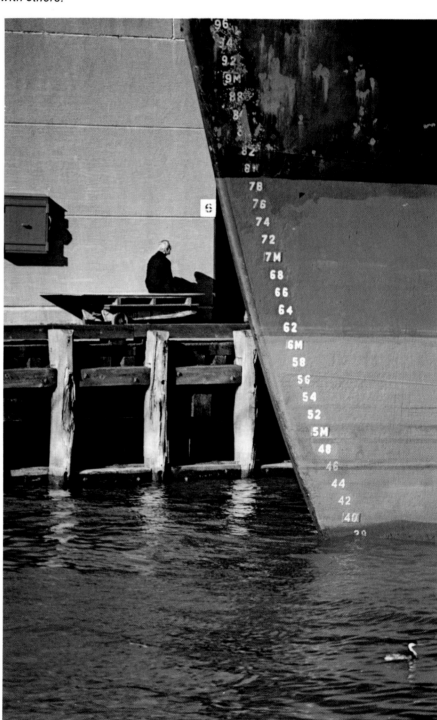

For years Spanish and Portuguese navigators coursed California's offshore waters. But thick fogs and jagged shorelines concealed a narrow gap in the mountain ridges behind which lay one of the greatest landlocked anchorages in the world. Not until 1769 was the magnificent harbor seen by anyone other than native Indians. A land expedition having overshot its objective of Monterey came upon it by chance. Though the group's leader—Gaspar de Portola—was more chagrined than awed, his chronicler, Padre Juan Crespi, wrote of ". . . an immense arm of the sea . . . which penetrated into the land as far as the eye could reach."

Because of the filling of its shallow waters that began during Gold Rush days, the big bay behind the Golden Gate isn't as immense as it once was, but the great harbor encompasses an impressive expanse of more than 400 square miles of water.

Three bays in one, San Francisco Bay is the waterway leading to the smaller San Pablo and Suisun Bays at the north and northeast. Within this maritime region is a waterfront complex made up of more than half a dozen distinct ports (San Francisco, Redwood City, Oakland, Alameda, Richmond, Benicia, Sacramento, Stockton) that handle products as exotic and varied as their worldwide markets. Cargos vary literally from soup to nuts, including wines and wood chips, aircraft parts and almonds.

SOMETIMES A MULTI-LEVEL VIGOR
A truck speeds north over the Golden Gate, a tanker steams west, and a gull matches speed and direction with an inbound sailboat.

DICK ROWAN

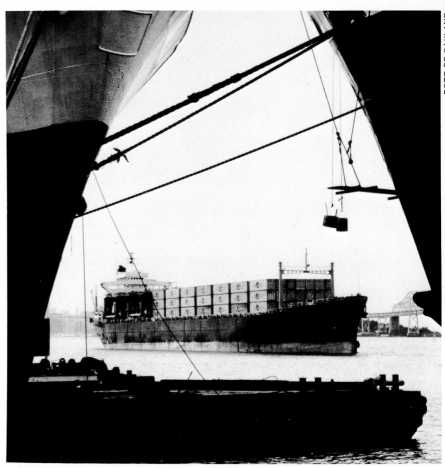

GLIMPSE OF YESTERDAY, TOUCH OF TODAY

Etched sharply against cottony clouds, below, San Francisco's skyline looks down at Hyde Street Pier's historical ship collection. Hardly giving the sparkling city a nod in passing, a sea-land container ship heads for berth at Port of Oakland, right, largest container port in the Pacific Basin.

"The ferries moved forty million commuters a year across the bay..."

Born and raised in Oakland, Harry Dring first went to sea in 1938. Since 1955 he has worked with San Francisco's Maritime State Historic Park, directing the restoration and preservation of historical ships once used in Pacific Coast commerce.

"At the Hyde Street Pier, we've decided that our ships are to represent the building period of 1890 to 1915 . . . the oldest one being built in '90 and the youngest in '15.

"We're not talking about pirate days, and we're not talking about yo-ho-ho sea chanteys and guys running around in pigtails and bell-bottom pants. The sailing ship master of this period wore a dark blue suit and a gold watch chain. The crew didn't wear monkey suits or uniforms. They looked like bums because they were bums, in a sense. Oh, there were plenty of good seamen among them, but they weren't dressed up in anything.

"You've got to put this thing in the right context and then be pretty hard-nosed about sticking to it. The Barbary Coast was certainly in existence in the '90's, and they were still shanghaiing sailors. But this tends to get out of hand; it gets too dramatic.

"Of course, we're also concerned with when the ships were used—with the nostalgia of the era. For example, the ferry steamer Eureka *was built in 1890, and she carried passengers until 1957. Do you know that in 1927 there were 40 million commuters a year—before the bridges —riding ferry boats across the bay? That's a hell of a lot of doughnuts and coffee.*

"Southern Pacific was running its own ferryboats. So were Santa Fe and Western Pacific. There was water transportation all over the place. You'd go to Vallejo on a ferryboat; you'd go to Richmond on a ferryboat; you'd go to Berkeley on a ferryboat. . . .

*"*Thayer *is a typical West Coast lumber schooner. She was built up in Eureka in 1895, and she carried lumber along the coast until steam schooners—like* Wapama—*took over.* Thayer *went codfishing up in the Bering Sea and continued to do so except for the war, when she was used as a barge. . . .*

"We have to take care of these ships so our children can see what it was all about. If they aren't taken care of, the worms eat them up. You know why we're having worm damage on our ships? Because the Bay is getting cleaner and the natural life is returning. I'm probably the only guy around who thinks there's some good in pollution. In the wooden ship days, they laid them up in the estuaries because the water there was so foul that nothing lived in it. . . .

"Sure, Thayer *carried lumber along the coast and so did* Wapama. *But once the trees were logged off near the coast they had to go farther inland. Well, the farther you got from the sea, the more expensive it was to get the logs to a ship. And as highways improved, the obvious thing was you went in and logged, and you hauled it out with trucks, and you milled it locally. Then it was shipped by trucks or train. A lot of northwest lumber comes down here today, but it's used way inland and not on the seacoast, so it just isn't practical any more to send much lumber by ship down the coast."*

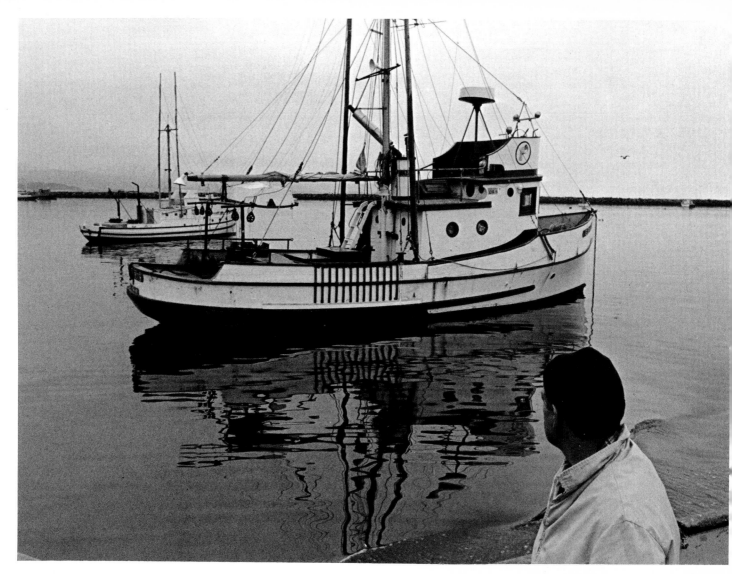

BY THE YAWN'S EARLY LIGHT
Party boats get an early but not always bright start on the day, heading out to fishing grounds long before the sun shows itself. Even with a gang aboard, the first couple of hours pass in sleepy silence.

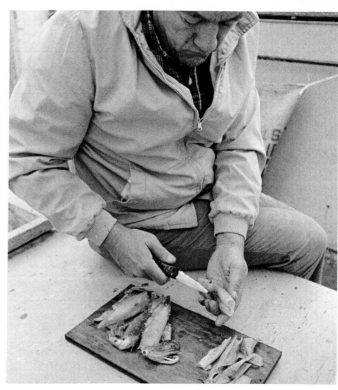

EYE-OPENING CHORE
To wile away time until lines go in the water, there's always bait cutting. Heads, eyes, and insides of squid are removed, and body is sliced into long strips.

SIDETRIP to sea, or stalking the LOGY lingcod

Stumbling out of bed at an outrageous hour, you somehow make it to the waterfront. There, you stand with your fishing gear at your feet, your hands in your pockets, wondering why. As the boat you've boarded chugs smoothly out of the chilly harbor, you huddle in a sheltered spot, and when it starts rolling in the open sea, you move closer to the rail.

After an hour or two, the engines shudder to silence. You bait up and let line run off the reel. You wait. Someone on the other side of the boat yells and reels in. There's a strike. And another. Just as you convince yourself that it isn't your day, a vibration runs all the way to your shoulders.

You crank in line—surely much more than you let out —until a form takes shape in the water. With the rod arcing wildly, you keep a tight line until someone swings the gaff. Breathing heavily, you look fondly at what must be a record catch and decide that, after all, everything was worthwhile.

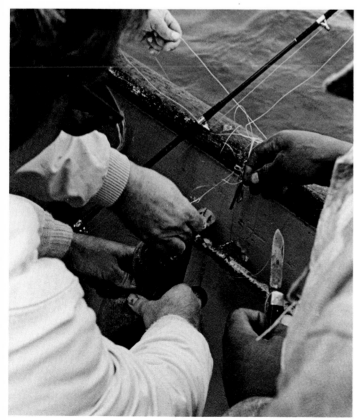

TRIBULATION . . . AND THE REWARD
When a dozen fishermen trail as many lines off one boat, fierce tangles are sure to occur, but hot tempers are soothed by cold beer. Sometimes the only answer is to cut the leader and start all over again. All else is forgotten when the big ones start hitting.

SEASIDE SPROUT ROUTE
Rolling past fields of broccoli, artichokes, and Brussels sprouts—and frequently providing easy access to such recreation areas as Pomponio Beach (top)—Cabrillo Highway stretches length of San Mateo coast. However, much agricultural acreage is being elbowed aside by creeping construction.

From ART to ARTICHOKES
along the San Mateo shore

Most of the San Mateo County coastline is open, unbuilt-upon country, and the greater part of the shore is publicly accessible. South of San Francisco, State 1 hurries through several clusters of creeping subdivisions (the ones that inspired the hit tune "Little Boxes"), cuts across some sheer cliffs (that in wet years occasionally let go, road and all), and then settles down to skirting a chain of fine beaches. Along the way are but a few towns —Pacifica, Montara, El Granada, Half Moon Bay—most of them actively engaged in fishing or with a fishing past. Galleries and seaside restaurants attract weekend visitors to some of the settlements, but a large part of coastside San Mateo is not recreation oriented, being given over to such fog-loving crops as artichokes, Brussels sprouts, or broccoli—and to dairy farms. As one eye-catching sign along the highway states: "Our cows are out standing in their field."

HITTING THE BEACH
THE HARD WAY
Winter winds battering the San Mateo coast often tear small boats from their moorings and hurl them ashore. At Princeton, hapless owners trench beneath a beached hull so they can work canvas slings around it to ease the boat out of danger.

HARVEST
IN THE HOLLOW

At Halloween, jumbles of pumpkins attract people from all over the San Francisco Peninsula to Half Moon Bay area. Candidates for jack-o'-lanterns make fall the most colorful time of the year.

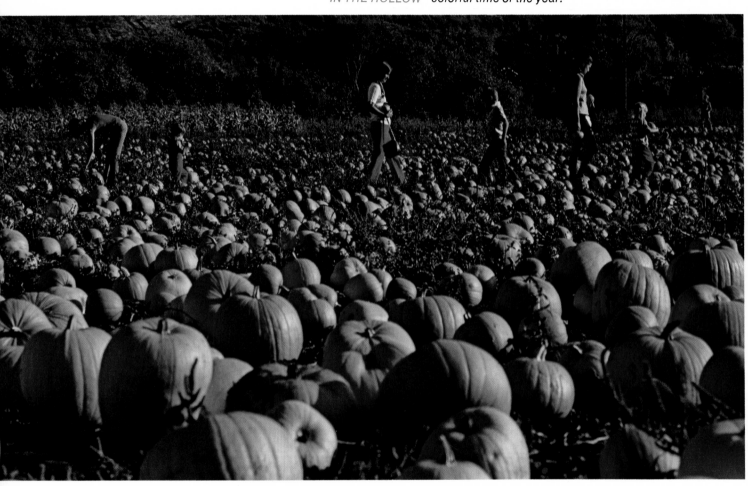

Without SEA LIONS, we'd have no trained SEAL acts

The voice of the coyote may be the most melodic sound to people who live in the desert, but coastal dwellers maintain that nothing compares with the hoarse bellow of a sea lion. Along much of California's coastline, roars, grunts, coughs, and barks—coming from several species of sea lions and seals—are sweet music to the ears of lovers of the shore.

Commonly seen swimming near shore or hauled out on rocks, members of the *Pinnipedia* (flipper-footed) order move on land by an ungainly squirming or humping motion. Most common species of seals cannot rotate their hind flippers, which extend behind the body like a tail. But the sea lion can accomplish this feat. And because of its comparative grace on land (as well as its intelligence) the female of the species is best known —trained to the ignominious job of entertaining people—as the performing "seal" you see at amusement parks.

WATER SPORTS
A familiar scene to coast watchers, sea lions cavort near shore, as clownlike in the wild as they appear in animal shows. Scuba divers frequently have freshly speared fish stolen from them by mischievous—and hungry—sea lions.

Elephant Seal. Males have bulbous snout, are brown or silver-gray; females are same color; 15-16 feet and to 5,000 pounds for males, 11 feet and 1,700 pounds for females. Seen at San Nicolas Island, off Santa Barbara; Año Nuevo Island.

Harbor Seal. Chunky shape, no external ears, squarish muzzle, backward-pointing hind flippers, mottled grayish color; size 5-6 feet and 250-300 pounds for males, slightly smaller for females. Seen in San Francisco Bay; at San Nicolas Island.

California Sea Lion. The trained "seal" of marine shows. Males dark brown, females light brown; 7-8 feet and 500-1,000 pounds for males, 6 feet and 200-600 pounds for females. Seen on Channel Islands off Santa Barbara; at Point Piedras Blancas, northern San Luis Obispo County.

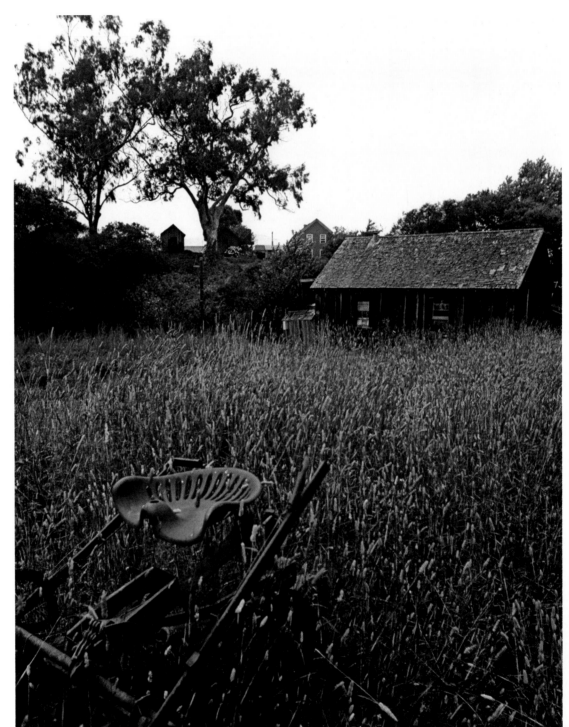

OUTSKIRTS OF TOWN
On a Spanish map dated April 16, 1839, Arroyo de San Gregorio is shown as part of San Gregorio land grant. In the late 1800s the village was a coastside resort, popular with sportsmen who jounced over the stage road from San Mateo.

San Gregorio – Pescadero
NOSTALGIC records of a BYGONE DAY

Their names are old world. Their look is old time. Their language is Portuguese—with English thrown in for the benefit of outsiders. Lying close to the coast, roughly 15 miles south of Half Moon Bay, San Gregorio and Pescadero are connected by a lovely portion of stage road that ambles over hill and down dale, more or less paralleling State 1.

Once a proverbial "popular resort," the town of San Gregorio (population 150) is today mainly a supply center for surrounding cattle and sheep ranches. Pescadero, with a population of about 1,000, is a more proper-appearing town, with tidy, New England-looking houses, a general store, a restaurant, a tavern, and several churches. A short distance from downtown is a strawflower factory, where locally grown *Helichrysum* are packed for shipment after being wired into bright bunches by women working in their own homes.

In these two gentle communities there is no such thing as a rush hour because there are no traffic lights and few cars . . . and no one is in a hurry to get anywhere.

CENTER OF TOWN
Today's town life centers around San Gregorio's post office and the general store, offering everything from saws to Portuguese sausage.

...PESCADERO

LIVELY FETE
With music, a parade, a livestock auction, and a barbecue, Pescadero is most active in May, during Chamarita—the Holy Ghost and Pentecost Festival. Spirited bidding takes place in front of I.D.E.S. Hall (initials stand for Portuguese words meaning Society for the Divine Holy Spirit), proceeds going to the local Catholic church.

MAIN STREET
Many years ago, legend says, a ship wrecked off Pigeon Point lost most of its cargo of white paint to Pescadero salvors, and the town has been using it ever since. A few steps across the road from Norm's is Duarte's Tavern and Restaurant, social hub of town and surrounding ranches.

SAFETY IN THE SEA
As in a stand of shoreside trees, the fronds and stems of Macrocystis, *giant bladder kelp, stretch up toward the sun. Growing as much as a foot a day to lengths of over 100 feet, forests of the great brown algae provide shelter for tremendous varieties of aquatic life.*

KELP–
spinach of
the sea

A familiar sight to California beachcombers are the matted tangles of greenish brown "seaweed" that lie strewn about the shore. Contrary to their common name, seaweeds are not weeds but algae—and they are very useful plants. Of the thousands of varieties of seaweed, about a dozen are used commercially. In Asia and Europe, certain types are eaten by humans as well as farm animals. In the United States, "Spinach of the Sea" has yet to be featured on a restaurant menu, but seaweed products are used as a jelling agent in canned meats, ice cream, cheeses, and candy. They are also used for medicinal purposes and in paints, auto polishes, and acoustic tiles. These products are made chiefly from the giant kelp that grows in enormous beds along the California coast. Because harvesting the kelp canopy has an environmental impact on marine populations that dwell in it, cutting is done under regulation of the California Fish and Game Commission to prevent depletion of this valuable natural resource.

SHELTER IN THE STRANDS
At the surface an otter waves a casual paw while wrapped in kelp to keep from drifting away; at the base a kelpfish peers out of his home in the holdfast (root system); on the ocean floor a spotted nudibranch snails his way through anemones clustered between kelp attachments.

BOB EVANS

BOB EVANS

St. George Reef
• CRESCENT CITY

N

Trinidad Head
Humboldt Bay
• EUREKA

Point Cabrillo
• FORT BRAGG

Point Arena
• POINT ARENA

Bodega Bay
Lightstation
• BODEGA BAY

Point Reyes
Farallon
• Point Blunt Lightstation

Point Bonita
SAN FRANCISCO

Pigeon Point
• SANTA CRUZ

Point Pinos
Monterey Lightstation
• MONTEREY

Point Sur

Piedras Blancas
• MORRO BAY

San Luis Obispo

NORTHERN CALIFORNIA'S CHAIN OF LIGHT

Twelfth Coast Guard District—headquartered in San Francisco—administers stations above Point Arguello, most of them land based. An exception is St. George Reef light, which perches on a sea-washed rock six miles out in the ocean.

California's earliest coastal navigation lights were probably an oil lamp placed in a cottage window or a lantern hung on an oar jammed into the sand. When lighthouses were first constructed on the west coast in the mid-1850s, their design was based on those long in operation in New England: a white tower rising from a tidy Cape Cod dwelling. The first station, installed in 1854 on Alcatraz Island, was followed by others around San Francisco. (Before construction could begin at the Farallon Islands, the Coast Guard had to send an armed party to reason with men who gathered sea bird eggs there and who were reluctant to let the builders land.)

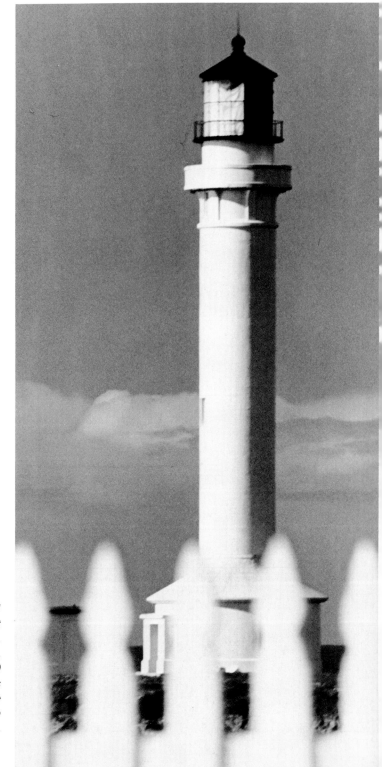

A CANDLE-LIKE BEACON

Housed in a reinforced concrete tower, Point Arena light is 115 feet above sea level. This is 35 feet lower than its predecessor, whose tower and lens—lighted in 1890 —were demolished in Northern California's 1906 earthquake. Window drapes are pulled during the day to keep sunlight off the lens.

Letting the
LIGHT shine forth

SOME SQUAT, OTHERS SOAR
Point Bonita light, left, crouches at north side of Golden Gate. In 1855 the station boasted the coast's first fog signal, a cannon that thundered into operation in August. By October the sergeant in charge was ready to desert his post, having—in three days—snatched only two hours's rest. Piedras Blancas light, below, thrusts skyward north of Morro Bay.

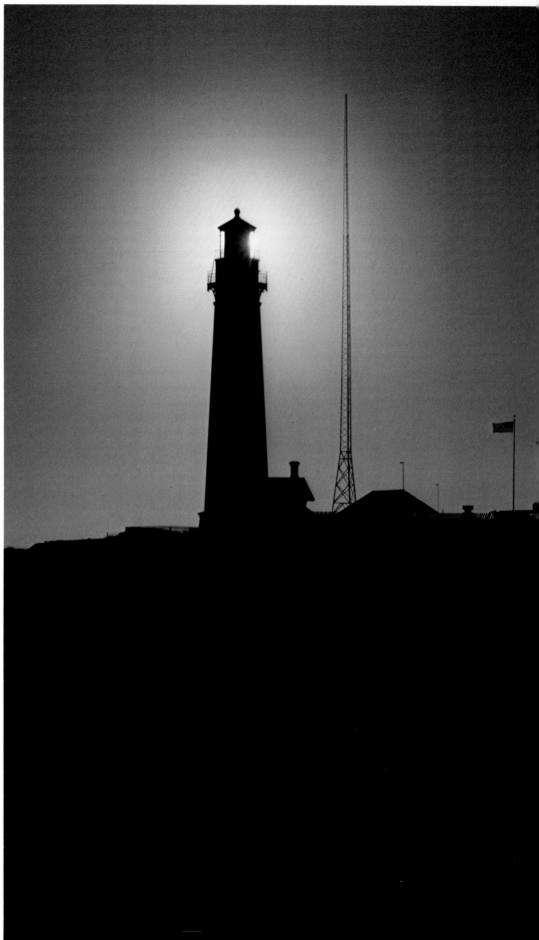

A LIGHT . . .

Stately Pigeon Point light is a landmark for motorists driving the coast highway between San Francisco and Santa Cruz. Named after Carrier Pigeon, *a ship that piled up twenty years before the station was installed, the light can be seen eighteen miles away.*

PETER CAPEN

Catadioptric prism

Dioptric prism

Lamp

Bull's eye

Dioptric prism

Catadioptric prism

... AND A LENS
Ring-shaped dioptric prisms refract light rays and catadioptric prisms reflect them, directing a beam along a single horizontal path. Sets of prisms and bull's eyes are arranged into a series of panels, as in the San Luis Obispo lens, left. When the entire lens revolves around a light source, an observer sees a concentration of rays, or a "flash."

FRAN COLEBERD

Locals claim that SANTA CRUZ is the SUNNY side of the bay

Santa Cruz is a little like an old shoe. Worn around the edges, a bit sprung at the seams, somewhat faded—but comfortable and loved. Residents, visitors, and even passersthrough sense a simple air, a down-to-earth hominess that contrasts with the elegance and polish of Monterey. It's an intriguing mixture of tiny summer cottages (most of them ancient), well groomed Victorian homes, and starkly modern structures.

The town has long been a San Francisco Bay Area summer tourist terminus. Locals take pride in pointing out that it's the climate that draws people to Santa Cruz and the adjoining towns of Capitola, Aptos, Rio del Mar. When fog sits over the inland valleys, Santa Cruz is almost sure to be sparkling. And during summer hot spells, San Jose folks head for you-know-where to cool off.

For further diversion (such as Pokerino, Skee Ball, and the Giant Dipper), everyone goes to the lovable old Boardwalk, one of the finest amusement parks left in the country. It's crowded to capacity in the summer. So are seven state parks and beaches spotted along the Santa Cruz shore, all offering a place in the sun.

NATURE IS THE ARCHITECT
Pressed in by a mobile home park on bluffs to the north and an expanding residential development to the south, tiny Natural Bridges State Park easily eludes first-time visitors. But once found, it's worth many return trips. The sandstone arches and crumbling cliffs are under constant attack by smashing waves.

MAN IS THE MAKER
Before hordes of people settle on Santa Cruz Beach, early-morning bikers savor a quiet moment near Municipal Wharf. Topside are gift shops, restaurants, fish markets. The wharf and an amusement park boardwalk fronting the beach offer diversions for fun seekers.

**FISH AND FUN
FOR EVERYONE**
*Once a port for ships loading produce from
Salinas Valley, Moss Landing is no less
busy today with action from fishing boats
and anglers, flower stalls and antique
shops. A huge power plant, looming like a
battleship over the harbor, startles
visitors, but some local citizens
like its sparkling night lighting.*

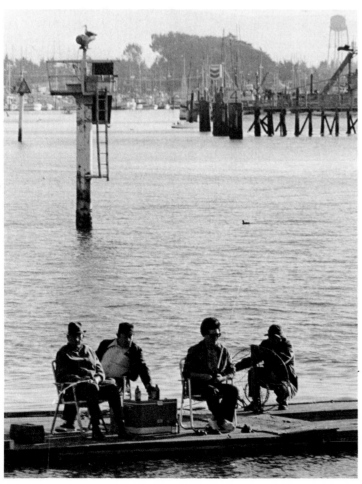

FLOWERS, fishing fleets, and a flurry of FLEA markets

In their defensible eagerness to push on to the good life in Monterey, motorists traveling along State 1 south from Santa Cruz usually hustle right through a coastal sector that may be less endowed with spectacular scenery than the Monterey Peninsula is, but which is important in many other ways. A cool, moist climate, with little damage from frost, makes the upper coastal corner of Monterey County one of the state's principal agricultural areas. Acres and acres of artichoke plants stud the fields (in Castroville a sign arching over the road proclaims that it's the artichoke capital of the world). And there are fields of strawberries, cauliflower, sugar beets, and lettuce— the crop that gives Salinas Valley the name "America's Salad Bowl."

Twisting inland from Moss Landing is a long, crooked arm of the sea—an estuary. One of the most important and most critical wetland resources in the state, Elkhorn Slough is a rich broth of life forms ranging from green algae to blue herons.

ZOOMING IN LOW
Near Castroville, self-styled artichoke capital of the world, a crop duster lays a swath of insecticide over a prickly field of "chokes."

AL LOWRY

Monterey

Monterey's recreational attractions are surpassed only by its scenic wonders. Together the two are a magnet drawing thousands of visitors annually to this wondrous peninsula. Here, nature's features are diverse and superb, from the dune country below the Salinas River to the white sand beaches of Asilomar and Carmel, from the stately pines of Del Monte Forest to the weathered cypresses of Point Lobos State Reserve.

Readily acccessible is the sea from above Monterey to Point Lobos. Farther south, the shore becomes less easy to reach because of steep cliffs, making the motoring experience the most popular attraction.
Since much of the Big Sur back country is protected as the Ventana Wilderness, many important biological communities flourish there, as well as along the shore. Caring little for boundaries, the California sea otter frolics north of its officially designated refuge well into Monterey Bay. Sea lions, seals, and sea birds breed in this region; kelp beds support fish, shellfish, and other invertebrates.

Below the Big Sur area, the shore curves inland to meet two stream valleys that converge in Morro Bay—one of the coast's largest estuaries. Representing "the shore" for much of San Luis Obispo County—and for communities as far east as Fresno—Pismo Beach and Avila Beach are as famous for sunning as they are for clamming and fishing. Between Pismo and Nipomo Dunes to the south stretches a long, jumbled coastline of sandy beaches and dunes.

South

Haunting Presence of the Ocean

. . . you can see the breakers leaping
high and white by day; at night the
outline of the shore is traced in
the transparent silver by the moonlight
and the flying foam; and from all
around, even in quiet weather, the
low, distant, thrilling roar of the
Pacific hangs over the coast. . . .

—Robert Louis Stevenson

Where the smooth sweep of the bay merges into the wooded headland, nature has worked with consummate skill. Rocky palisades alternate with sandy beaches. Cypress-covered hillsides converge with the ocean's edge. The climate is benign, the air crystalline. The peninsula's three towns—Monterey, Pacific Grove, and Carmel—have grown considerably since the scenery inspired the setting of Robert Louis Stevenson's *Treasure Island.* But an enlightened development company has preserved many acres of forest and shore in much the same condition as they were when first seen by the Spaniards in 1542.

SURF, sand, and forest – the MONTEREY Peninsula

THE SUPERLATIVE SHORE
"Magnificent panoramas ... incomparable
beauty . . . spectacular scenery. . . ."
Extravagance abounds in descriptions of the
Monterey coastline. But hyperbole
seems justified when attempting to verbalize
the vision of such places as Spanish Bay,
along famed Seventeen-Mile Drive.

...MONTEREY

MOOD AT WEATHER'S WHIM
Thin fog isolates a salmon troller lying
motionless in midsummer Monterey harbor.
At edge of the autumn ocean, below, waves
explode against Lover's Point, and every
detail of land and sea snaps into clear focus.

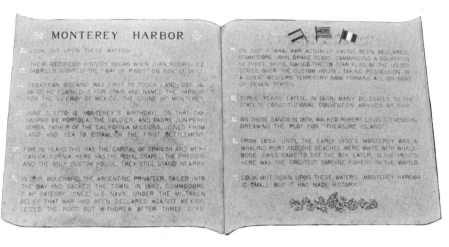

HARBOR UNDER THREE FLAGS
Plaque recording Monterey's multicultural
history is near entrance to Fisherman's
Wharf, town's number one tourist attraction.
Wharf's ancient planks and pilings
resound to constant footsteps, but casual
visitors seldom view its lovably
seedy water side.

DICK ROWAN

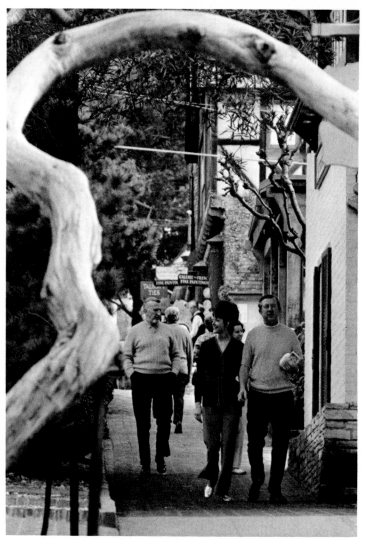

CULTIVATING THE CASUAL AIR
Elf-forest architecture of Carmel-by-the-Sea has its detractors, but this tidy settlement south of Monterey enjoys an offhand atmosphere that draws year-round visitors from afar. Sandy crescent of Carmel's beaches invites sun bathers and strollers even in winter.

"Monterey is...the pleasantest and most civilized looking place in California."

In 1834-1836 and in 1859-1860, Richard Henry Dana voyaged along the California coast. His experiences—set down in the book *Two Years Before the Mast* —vividly document part of the history of what was then a remote Mexican province.

BANCROFT LIBRARY

"The bay of Monterey is very wide at the entrance, being about twenty-four miles between the two points, Ano Neuvo at the north, and Pinos at the south, but narrows gradually as you approach the town, which is situated in a bend, or large cove, at the south-eastern extremity, and about eighteen miles from the points, which makes the whole depth of the bay. The shores are extremely well wooded (the pine abounding on them), and as it was now the rainy season, everything was as green as nature could make it—the grass, the leaves, and all; the birds were singing in the woods, and great numbers of wild fowl were flying over our heads. . . . We came to anchor within two cable lengths of the shore, and the town lay directly before us, making a pretty appearance. . . . The red tiles . . . on the roofs, contrasted well with the white plastered sides, and with the extreme greenness of the lawn upon which the houses—about a hundred in number—were dotted about, here and there, irregularly. There are in this place, and in every other town which I saw in California, no streets, or fences (except here and there a small patch was fenced in for a garden), so that the houses are placed at random upon the green, which, as they are of one story and of the cottage form, gives them a pretty effect when seen from a little distance. . . .

"The Mexican flag was flying from the little square, whitewashed Presidio, and the drums and trumpets of the soldiers, who were out on parade, sounded over the water, and gave great life to the scene. Every one was delighted with the appearance of things. We felt as though we had got into a Christian (which in the sailor's vocabulary means civilized) country.

"Monterey, as far as my observation goes, is decidedly the pleasantest and most civilized-looking place in California. . . . The houses . . . are of one story, built of clay made into large bricks, about a foot and a half square and three or four inches thick, and hardened in the sun. . . . Some of the more wealthy inhabitants have glass to the windows and board floors; and in Monterey nearly all the houses are plastered on the outside. The better houses, too, have red tiles upon the roofs. . . .

"In Monterey there are a number of English and Americans (English or 'Ingles' all are called who speak the English language) who have married Californians, become united to the Catholic church, and acquired considerable property. Having more industry, frugality, and enterprise than the natives, they soon get nearly all the trade into their hands. . . .

"Nothing but the character of the people prevents Monterey from becoming a great town. The soil is as rich as man could wish; climate as good as any in the world; water abundant, and situation extremely beautiful. The harbor, too, is a good one, being subject only to one bad wind, the north; and though the holding-ground is not the best, yet I heard of but one vessel's being driven ashore here.

SEA OTTERS
are not surviving...
they're THRIVING

When Lewis and Clark reached the Pacific, they took note of the "sea-orter pole-cats" whose coats were so thick and silky. Their matter-of-fact report brought an invasion of American fur hunters, who continued down the coast the mass slaughter of otters already occurring off Alaska and Canada. Through the 1800s, a few undiscovered animals along the shores of Big Sur country somehow held out against extinction. Today, over 1,200 California otters gambol in the coastal reserve that stretches 100 miles south from Monterey. A sea otter's appetite is rapacious, and its favorite food is shellfish—particularly abalone. Surfacing with its prey and a rock, the otter balances them on his belly and then dashes them together to break open the shell. Commercial abalone fishermen complain that the multiplying otters are destroying their livelihood, but the animal's defenders point out that otters inhabited the entire Pacific coast before man decimated their population.

"GO GET YOUR OWN LUNCH!"
Sleek from a snack-gathering trip to the bottom, an otter munches remains of an abalone, calmly fending off an eager gull who believes in sharing the spoils.

DICK ROWAN

142

"HEY! WHO ARE YOU?"
Looking every bit a grizzled gentleman, an otter raises his hind flipper and regards the portrait photographer. Intensely curious and nonaggressive, otters will let skindivers approach to within a couple of feet before diving. Unlike other species, the California sea otter spends almost all of its life in water, seldom coming ashore.

Map

Santa Cruz

Point Lobos — Monterey

Point Sur

N

Point Lopez

Point Piedras Blancas — San Simeon
Cambria
Cayucos

WHERE TO SEE A SEA OTTER
Sea otters range from Alaska well down the Baja California coast, but numbers of the California otter are greatest from about Monterey Bay to just north of Morro Bay. In areas shown, they are usually observed bobbing around in kelp beds.

143

A BEACH
is sand
on the move

Beaches are dynamic creations of winds, waves, and currents. Responding to the slightest change in these shaping forces, a beach face constantly remolds itself, seeking equilibrium. Pockets of beach between cliff and sea that are typical of Northern California indicate a youthful, rising shore; erosion and sediment transport have barely begun. Wave action gradually straightens a shoreline, letting currents deposit continuous stretches of sand, as in Southern California. As more inland dams impound the major supplies of new sand and more breakwaters disturb sand-carrying currents, dredging and hauling must be resorted to in order to maintain what were once natural beaches.

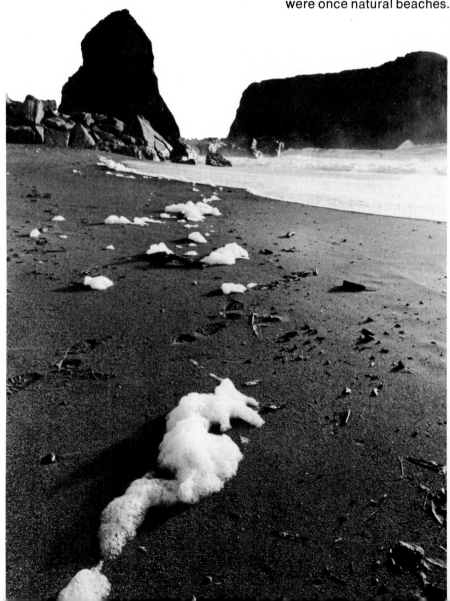

ONE DAY IT'S SAND...
Smooth sand beaches are the result of sea cliff erosion and of rivers and streams bringing quartz particles directly to the shore. Though such beaches lose sand to wave action, they are replenished by currents that run parallel to the coast— usually in a north-south direction—carrying sand grains with them.

. . . THE NEXT DAY
IT'S ROCKS   A beach is a fragile and fluid thing. Cobbles pave many shores
where storm waves or natural transport have removed sand
grains. But rocky beaches can also result from manmade
breakwaters or marinas, which reroute the southern drift
and—by stopping new sand from coming in to the
beach—prevent beach recovery.

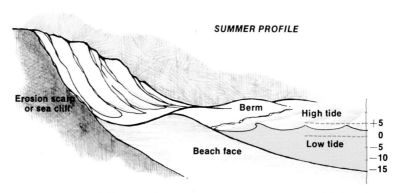

SUMMER PROFILE

Erosion scarp or sea cliff

Berm

High tide

Beach face

Low tide

+5
0
—5
—10
—15

A BEACH IN SUMMER
In summer, gentle wave action lifts grains
from the underwater beach face and
nudges them shoreward, piling sand into a
low terrace called a berm. As typified
by Zuma Beach (north of Santa Monica),
below, the summer berm is wide, most
of it beyond reach of all but the biggest
high-tide waves. This is the part of the beach
where sun bathers frolic.

WINTER PROFILE

Erosion scarp
or sea cliff

Berm   High tide   +10
                                  +5

Beach face   Bar   Low tide   0
                                  -5
                                  -10
                    Bar   -15
              Trough

A BEACH IN WINTER
In winter, larger waves that strike shore
more closely together nibble away at
the berm, tumbling sand out to deeper
water where it forms bars. In some areas
—such as Oceanside (San Diego County),
above—rough winter surf removes great
amounts of berm sand. Low tide then exposes
heavier rocks that tend to resist shifting.

Point Lobos: The Greatest Meeting of Land and Water

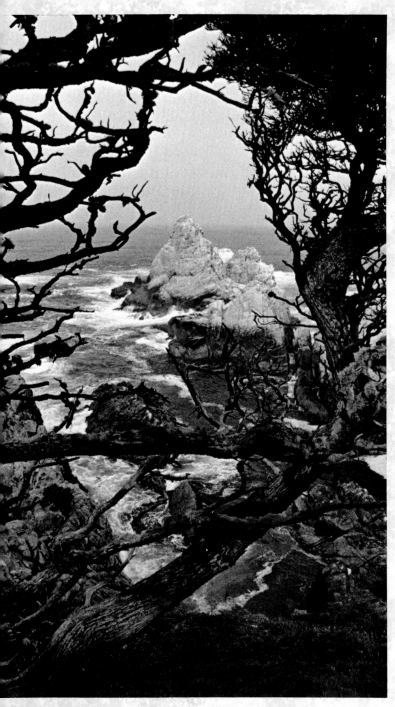

The many-fingered promontory of Point Lobos has survived the abuses of man almost intact. At various times before the state acquired it in 1933, cattle grazed the meadows, some parts were plowed for farming, and people with an eye for scenic homesites proposed a town on the knolls and ridges. Today, Point Lobos and 750 acres of surrounding sea floor comprise a reserve that is carefully regulated to remain a wild place for wild things.

An extravagant 300 plant species and 250 bird and animal species appear here in their seasons. Sea otters, sea lions, and migrating gray whales are frequently seen offshore; brown pelicans, diving cormorants, loons, and gulls reside on rocky islets. Springtime brings a crazy quilt of buttercups, lupine, poppy, and other wildflowers.

The best of Point Lobos must be explored by foot trail. Along the south shore, low tide exposes a fertile intertidal zone. The north side of the peninsula has ghostly groves of the vanishing Monterey cypress. Paths in the interior lead from open fields into dense stands of tall pines.

THE EVER-CHANGING LAND
Northernmost point in the reserve, guano-frosted Pinnacle Rock takes full impact of wind and wave but dissipates their force only slightly. Interaction between sea and shore is a natural process whose effects are dramatically apparent in this place protected from the not-always-helpful hand of man.

No one tidies the unkempt forest floor or trims the ungainly trees. The only accord is that of nature, a silent harmony into which man must fit himself.

THE NEVER-RESTING SEA
Sometimes gently washing against the shore, sometimes relentlessly battering it, the ocean surges over the rocks of China Cove.

SCENE TO THE SOUTH
North Shore Trail—one of the most spectacular strolls—gives glimpses over Bluefish Cove of a distant Carmelite monastery. It is one of the few signs of man visible from the reserve.

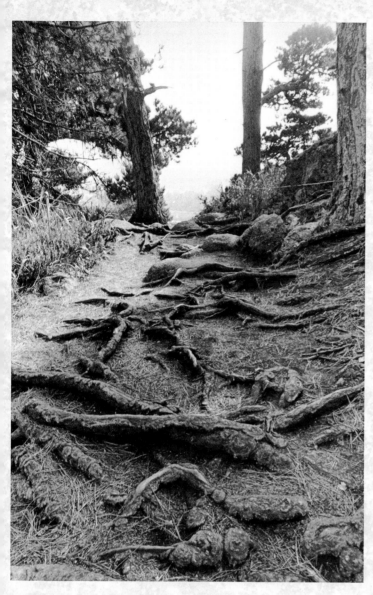

**TENACIOUS IN LIFE,
DIGNIFIED IN DEATH**
*Once widely distributed, the Monterey
cypress is making a last stand at Point Lobos.
Because foot traffic compacts earth
around tree roots, park trails are periodically
rerouted to give areas a chance to return
to their natural state.*

A wild coast and lonely–
BIG SUR COUNTRY

South of Point Lobos, the brooding Santa Lucia Mountains shoulder close to the sea. As if in retaliation, the Pacific throws its weight against the cliffs, creating the mist and thunder that haunt this solitary place. The remoteness of Big Sur has delayed human intrusion. So have its capricious weather and rugged terrain. The few people who inhabit this part of the coast are an independent breed, in turn inspired and overpowered by the Olympian grandeur surrounding them. On one side of State 1 lies roiling ocean; on the other is primordial mountain forest that encompasses the southernmost stands of coast redwoods. Persistent summer fogs sifting into canyons that are gilded by sunsets over an iridescent sea are commonplace, almost surreal occurrences in this uncommon country.

THE BRIDGE AT BIXBY CREEK
Almost hidden by hills and headlands, the graceful center span of Bixby Bridge arches 260 feet over a deep gorge. Twisting and curling for some fifty miles, the coast highway is slow driving but one of the most scenic north-south routes in California.

THE SEA AT
SADDLE ROCK
Only thirteen miles south of Big Sur post office is Julia Pfeiffer Burns State Park. One of its trails overlooks a waterfall that plunges straight down into the ocean. Park was once a grand estate, and many garden walls remain, half-hidden by wild growth.

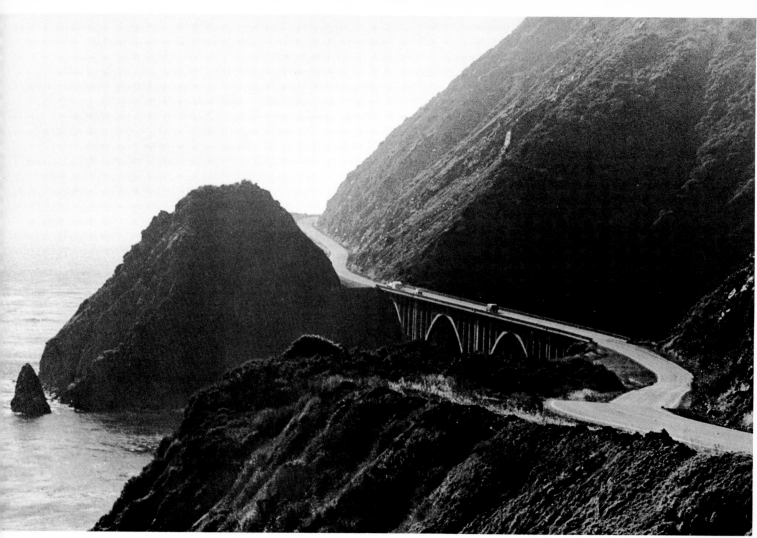

WHERE ARE ALL THE PEOPLE?

In a fifty-mile stretch of the Big Sur live only about 500 people. Winter washouts and landslides often obliterate portions of the precarious highway, making homes—most of them well concealed anyway—even more inaccessible. Occasional mailboxes along the highway are about the only evidence of habitation.

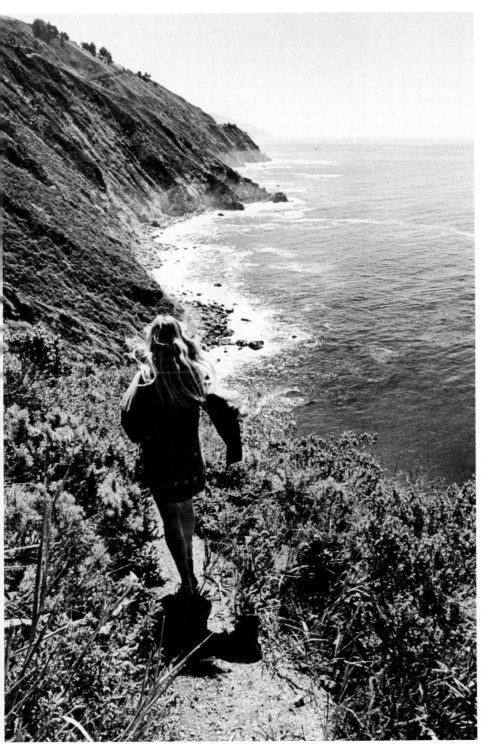

**WHO LIVES
IN THE BIG SUR?**
*Contrary to legend, there is no "art colony,"
since working artists who settle here
generally keep to themselves, as do ranchers
who live back in the hills. Residents and
guests of Esalen Institute—a cultural center
dedicated to expanding the human potential
—roam the coastline, getting close to nature.*

WILDLIFE
is the coast's
ENVIRONMENTAL
barometer

Bittern

Field mouse

Green frog

Though examples of wildlife extinction by slaughter are spectacular, only a few of the species listed by the government as rare or endangered have declined at the hand of the hunter. Most are victims of extensive habitat disruption and pollution. As man bulldozes coastal wetlands, meadows, and forests for homesites and industries and discharges his waste into the air and ocean, wildlife diminishes.

Even the most confirmed city dweller depends on food and uncontaminated water from the same lands and waters that harbor most wildlife. A few species—squirrels, gulls, opossums, raccoons—can adapt to man's altered environment, and their presence should not be taken as a sign of a healthy ecological balance. Instead, the increase of stillborn sea lion pups and the fruitless nesting of brown pelicans should serve as harbingers of potential disaster for man.

With the exception of the going-away water snake, which was captured on film by Ray Higgs, all photos below are by Tom Myers.

Water snake

Buck deer

Brown owl

Just a little guest HOUSE... with a CASTLE in the basement

On childhood trips to the 240,000-acre family ranch, William Randolph Hearst became so enamored of the site they used as a campground that, when he inherited the property in 1919, he built a considerably more permanent living quarters on the spot: a $50 million complex from which to govern his newspaper empire. Many of the rooms of the main house and the three guest houses—146 rooms in all—were specifically designed to hold pieces of Hearst's astounding collection of European art and antiques, estimated to be worth at least as much as the buildings themselves. (Rumor has it that there is still a dismantled castle in the basement of the main house.) For over a quarter of a century, construction materials and skilled artisans, as well as treasured objets d'art, arrived by steamer at the dock in the whaling village of San Simeon.

Hearst's acquisitive tendencies didn't stop with newspapers and art treasures. To entertain his many prominent guests, he fenced off 2,000 rolling acres for a private zoo. Then he gathered wild animals from around the world to fill it. Though the zoo was later closed, herds of zebra, elk, and Barbary sheep still roam the nearby hills.

Today the Enchanted Hill—as Hearst called it—is a State Historical Monument. For a few hours, anyone who can afford the entrance fee can experience vicariously the opulence of a life style in which money was no object.

The incredible antiques seem as endless as the tremendous, sweeping vistas of ocean and mountains. The view from the estate itself is of an untamed land. But the visitor parking lot below is often packed with cars and tour buses, and just below San Simeon, wild coast begins to give way to civilization. A clutter of neon signs on establishments catering to the castle crowds hints of the development to be repeated on a grand scale farther south.

THE OWNER'S FAVORITE ROOM
Gleam of antique silver is reflected in polished walnut of Refectory's monastic dining table. The magnificent stone overmantel of fireplace rises all the way to a 400-year-old ceiling, which is a series of elaborate, high-relief carvings.

**HIS WORKING LIBRARY
. . . AND A PLACE TO SWIM**
Gothic Library, below, was part of Hearst's personal suite where he did much of his work. Interior of Roman Pool room, left, is inlaid with acres of Venetian glass and gold tiles.

A BOON
FOR BOAT WATCHERS
"Fishing around here has dropped way off," some experts state in gloomy tones. But Morro Bay always seems filled with tidy vessels, many from other Western ports. Below are depicted some of the types of working craft that traverse this part of the coast.

Bottom Trawler. Drags a net along ocean floor to catch rock cod, sole, red snapper, halibut, shrimp. A good portion of fish taken off the coast are caught by trawlers.

Salmon Troller. Drags bait or moving lures from long, flexible outriggers to catch ocean salmon, fishing from April through September for this finest of coastal game fishes.

Trawlers, trollers, and a ROCK called MORRO

"Fishing's not what it used to be," said the man at the Chamber of Commerce, the corners of his mouth turning down. "But it's bound to get better," he concluded with smiling optimism.

People at Morro Bay fish for almost everything, and the community promotes its charm as a fishing village. Shoreside anglers cast for perch and flounder from piers, beaches, and rocky coast. Low tide finds clammers scratching in the sand. Oysters thrive here—more than 1,000 acres of them—and Morro Bay celebrates their contribution to the local economy each year with a weekend oyster festival. Visitors can wander through the beds and pluck their own bivalves to take home or sample them on the spot in a ready-made stew.

Many commercial and party fishing boats tie up behind the long, sandy spit that protects the harbor. Their creaking ropes, the screaming gulls, and the summer fog combine to create an atmosphere much like that of a New England seacoast town. Looking seaward toward Morro Rock, the 567-foot dome that stands at the entrance to the bay, the picturesque setting is complete, but looking toward shore, the soaring stacks of a power plant claim the dubious distinction of being almost as high as the rock itself.

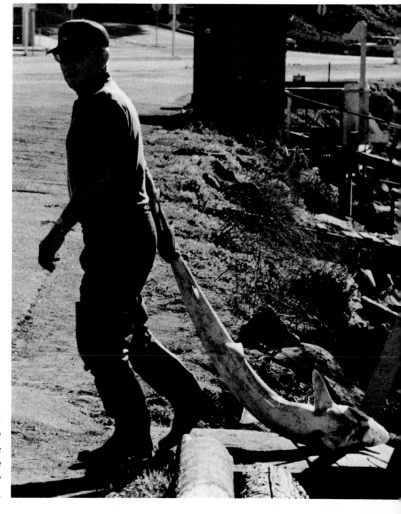

TAKING IT HOME
Fisherman drags a small shark for his own table up boat ramp. Some fish fanciers sniff at the idea of eating shark, not realizing that it is sold in the markets under several popular fish names.

Gill Netter. Sets out a series of nets on ocean floor, leaves them overnight, then returns the next day to haul in catches of sea bass, halibut, cod, and other bottom dwellers.

Albacore Boat. Scatters pieces of oily fish (called chum) to attract albacore and tuna, which are then caught on lines. Albacore boats make up one of coast's largest fleets.

...MORRO BAY

THE HARBOR
AND THE HILLS

With high hopes, gulls wait for a gill netter to chug its way across the lagoon. Bay's backdrop of San Luis Range blends 1,500-foot-high hills of Montana de Oro (Mountain of Gold) State Park, known for its bright springtime displays of California poppy.

**QUIET DAY
IN THE BAY**
Between ocean runs, nets are spread on deck or dock for mending. Their brilliance in the water doesn't seem to spook fish. Nor does fog deter a pier fisherman and his feathered friend.

Prehistoric dunes have left their mark everywhere along the coast, but California's shoreline today offers only a few hospitable pockets that combine the right elements for dune formation. The 15 miles of shore between Pismo Beach and Point Sal is one such place. There, the Santa Maria River brings down an abundant supply of sand, and the broad river valley invites the prevailing west wind to blow inland freely, sculpting the sand into waves as it passes.

A dune begins when onshore breezes pick up grains of dry sand from the beach face and carry them landward, where they may lodge against vegetation and form a hill. If nothing stops it, a dune will slowly crawl inland as its sand is blown up the windward slope, over the crest, and down the leeward side. As a hill moves, another forms in its place.

Where vegetation can gain a foothold, dune movement is slowed and often checked. A few hardy plants—such as sedge and ice plant—can withstand the burning salt wind on the seaward side of a dune, sending their anchoring roots deep into the sand. Once pioneer plants have taken hold, others begin growing in the dune's protected lee. These, in turn, attract hungry deer and provide homes for small wildlife.

Still, the stability of the dunes rests on a fragile balance. Vehicles and too many trampling feet can destroy that balance, causing sand accumulated over a thousand years to blow away in a decade.

WRITINGS ON THE SAND
Looking as if made by a pair of purposeful creatures walking arm in arm, tiny tracks stitch across wind-formed sand waves, above. Nearer the shore, sand ripples blend into barrier dune, right, sparsely grown with vegetation because of increasing amounts of salt in the air.

ED COOPER

164

SAND dune country – the land between two WORLDS

MODERATING NATURE'S FORCES

In dune areas where sand threatens to reclaim its own, man slows the process by planting beach grasses and shrubs. Snow fences and other artificial barriers look impressive but are not too effective in stabilizing shifting sands.

VROOM! VROOM!
Spewing sand and
bellowing like a wrathful
bull, a high-style vehicle
roars up the face of a
barrier dune. Guadalupe
area, just south of
Pismo Beach, is noted for
its Saharalike drifts.
Countless off-the-road
enthusiasts race over the
mounds aboard pillow-
tired contraptions that only
a dune buggy driver
could love.

PICKEREL/DANDELET

BOOM! BOOM!
Happy from the hunt, a trio takes a final look
around Oso Flaco Lake, left—in the heart
of Guadalupe dune country—before calling
it a day. At a quieter time, a belly flopper, above,
finds pleasure in his own way.

It's supposed to be
the CLAM CAPITAL
of the world

At Pismo Beach, you can pay a dollar and dig right in. That's all it costs to hunt the sweet-tasting clam that has brought fame to its namesake town. The circular, thick-shelled mollusks live all along the surf-swept sand beaches of the central coast, but they thrive at Pismo, where the sea floor slopes gradually for a long distance. The town has not been remiss in capitalizing on its good fortune. For 30 years it has scheduled a midwinter clam bash to coincide with minus tides, when the best catches are found on infrequently exposed sections of beach. Scores of dungaree- and sneaker-clad clammers come to turn the sand with spades or special rakes. A resident clammer summed up the feelings of local folk: "Everyone thinks the name is hilarious, but they sure come here when they want clams."

YOU CAN'T GET MUCH CLOSER
Pismo's hardpacked beach is an invitation to drive right down to water's edge for a bit of surf casting. Sand and salt may not be the best treatment for a car, but drivers who stay on damp hardpack—out of reach of waves—aren't likely to become stuck.

CATERING TO THE BIGGEST DRAWING CARD

The greatest abundance of clams on California's coast is found at Pismo Beach, and shoreside stores, below, provide everything for their capture, including quick haul-out for stranded motorists. At low tides the bivalve bides his time about five inches below the surface, within easy reach of a clam fork. Gauge on handle assures that catch is legal size of 4½ inches at its widest point.

It's not hard to see why the Spanish padres chose the pleasant valley of the Santa Ynez River to establish two missions; the land is fertile and the climate beneficent. La Purisima Concepcion Mission, near Lompoc, prospered under these conditions. Although the mission gradually disintegrated after being secularized in the 1830s, a faithful and complete replica has been built on the foundations of the original. Today, exuberant fields of flowers grow where the mission livestock grazed. Uninterrupted sun from May to September helps produce half of the flower seeds grown in the world.

Turn off the highway to FLOWER fields and MISSION trails

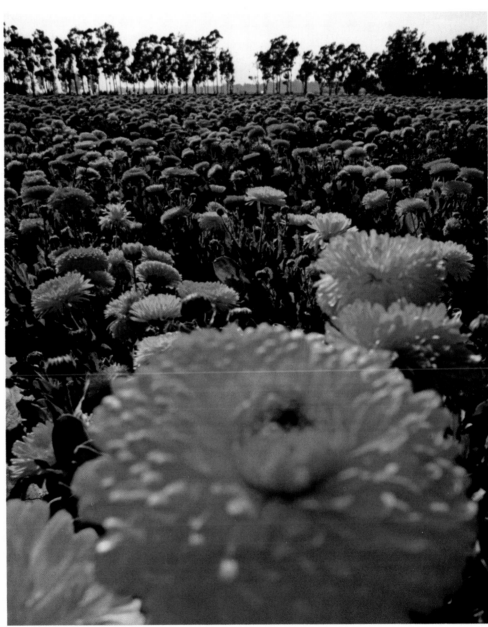

FLOWERS TO FILL THE EYE
It's late afternoon near Lompoc, and field workers take a final stroll down furrows of ageratum, looking for weeds. Brilliant calendulas, right, are raised for cut flowers, as well as for seed.

ALONG THE KING'S HIGHWAY

Spidery conjunction of two highways near
Lompoc forms a triangular loop that takes
in acres of flower fields (biggest ones are
indicated on map by blossoms) and
La Purisima Mission, above. In front of main
buildings of mission settlement can be seen a
segment of original El Camino Real footpath.

IN THE QUIET
OF THE CAPTAIN'S QUARTERS
Nosegay of wildflowers adds cheery note to
a Spartan table setting in La Purisima Quarters
Building, where officers and enlisted men
were housed. The wood-and-wrought-iron
light fixture is one of several hanging
in main church and chapel.

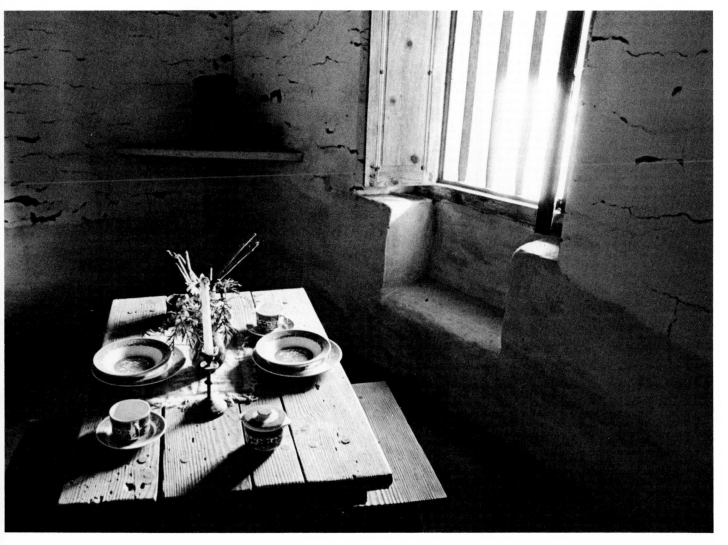

California's coast can be a CRUEL coast

As any sailor worth his salt knows, the Pacific isn't always what its name implies. Like any other ocean, it has its share of foul and foggy weather, and mariners unfortunate or unwise enough to be caught out of port when the sea is in a nasty mood had best give a wide berth to California's ragged western edge. Point Reyes claimed the state's first recorded shipwreck; in 1595 a sudden southeaster blew the galleon of Rodriquez Cermeno onto a reef. Since then, California waters have chewed up hundreds of ships. Cape Mendocino, Trinidad Head, Point Joe, Point Arguello, Point Fermin—all have taken their toll. But nowhere have there been more disasters than around the Santa Barbara Channel, where the convergence of two climates and various currents at Point Conception stir up especially fearful seas. At any one time almost anywhere along the California coast, at least a couple of battered hulks lie stranded on bars.

SAD SAGAS OF THE SEA
Schooner Mabel Gray, *above, went aground at Redondo Beach in 1904, losing her deck cargo of lumber, her masts, and her dignity. In 1923, Point Arguello was the scene of one of the U.S. Navy's greatest peacetime disasters. Unknowingly off course, a squadron of destroyers piled up on the rocks, right, losing 7 ships and 22 lives.*

BOOM! . . . AND BUST

Steamship Rosecrans, *taking a smashing broadside from the sea after running aground near Santa Barbara in 1912, top left, was battered, but she survived. Less lucky was the schooner* Venus, *bottom right; despite taut spring lines, she was broken apart by heavy seas off the mouth of Navarro River. Bottom left, a 100-ton sperm whale and* Ohioan *were fortuitously beached together at San Francisco's Lands End in 1937. Neither recovered.*

Coastal Santa

South of secretive Vandenberg Air Force Base and its ocean-oriented Pacific Missile Range, Point Arguello pokes a rocky finger out into the sea. Twenty miles farther along the shore, Point Conception follows suit by jutting sharply westward. These bold landforms mark a kind of magical zone in the California coast, for, political boundaries notwithstanding, the sector between them is a definite dividing line between Northern California and Southern California.

At Point Arguello the shore's westerly thrust diverts cold, south-coursing ocean currents away from the land. Rough seas, high winds, and fogs pushing down from the north are effectively blocked or broken up. Beyond Point Conception, the shore makes an abrupt turn to the east. This different lay of the land allows the earth to absorb more of the sun's rays, and the decided western slope of the coastal Santa Ynez Range acts like a giant mirror, reflecting solar energy southward.

Below the 34th parallel, rocky, hard earth suitable as livestock range changes to rich, fertile soil that supports citrus and avocado culture. Chaparral and pine are replaced by palms and other temperate-climate vegetation. The longer sloping coastal shelf smooths waves, and its shallows tempt surfers and sun bathers. As striking a difference as any is evident in Southern California's coastal architecture. Whitewashed walls, red tile roofs, and black ironwork speak not only of local pride in a Spanish heritage but of a more relaxed, languorous life style.

Barbara

reserving the Placid Air

In the afternoon they came into a
  land,
In which it seemed always afternoon.
All around the coast the languid
  air did swoon.

> —Alfred, Lord Tennyson

SANTA BARBARA
has a different kind
of life STYLE

To the Spaniards who settled this pocket of California in the late 18th century, it was a new land, a land different from their point of origin. Yet something about the blue skies and the bright waters reminded them of home, and they called their new abode "La Tierra Adorada"—the beloved land. Great ranches surrounded the area, and a gracious cultured life developed that made Santa Barbara the social capital of early California.

As 20th century newcomers discover and old-timers insist, Santa Barbara *is* different. Its setting is out of a storybook: fertile mountains to one side, a chain of scenic islands to the other. The climate is superb—more tropical than farther north, more temperate than farther south. Even the long, narrow coastline defies convention. Instead of running north-south like most of California, it stretches east-west. Reflecting its Mediterranean heritage, the prevailing architecture is white-walled, tile-roofed Spanish Colonial. Flowers and greenery prevail. Even the freeway that skirts the town is tropically landscaped.

Santa Barbara didn't just happen. Long ago its citizens realized that if the place was to remain "La Tierra Adorada," people were going to have to work to keep it that way. Most critical issues—such as comprehensive planning, redevelopment, pollution—are targets of citizen action. Like few other cities, Santa Barbara is a place where people are interested—and involved.

"It's not a matter of fighting city hall, here," said a developer. "It's getting along with civic-minded groups that really do their homework. Our own work is cut out for us, but the place shows it in its life style."

MEDITERRANEAN MOOD
Symbols of southern shore, fan palms stand sentinel-tall along Santa Barbara's shoreline, dividing beach from business district. Protected by the Channel Islands to the south and the Santa Ynez Mountains to the north, the city and its environs are blessed year-round by an equable climate.

ANDALUSIAN AMBIENCE
Tiled corridors and curved staircases of
County Courthouse, above, are but a small
part of this exquisite Spanish-Moorish
"palace." The theme echoes softly in the
flagstone courtyards of El Paseo, left, a
picturesque shopping arcade
evocative of old Spain.

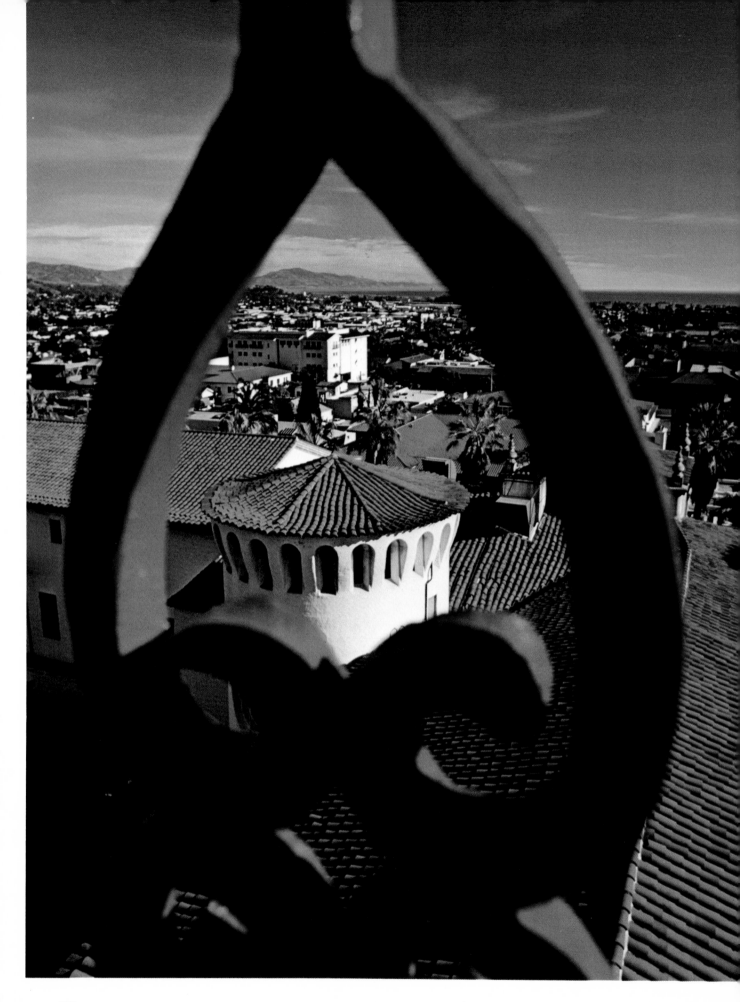

A CITY WITH STYLE
When residents speak of their city's style, they are referring not only to a happy potpourri of Spanish Colonial, Mexican, and Moorish architecture but also to a gracious and comfortable manner of living. Santa Barbara is not the typical "tourist town." First-time visitors remember their stay as a most civilizing experience.

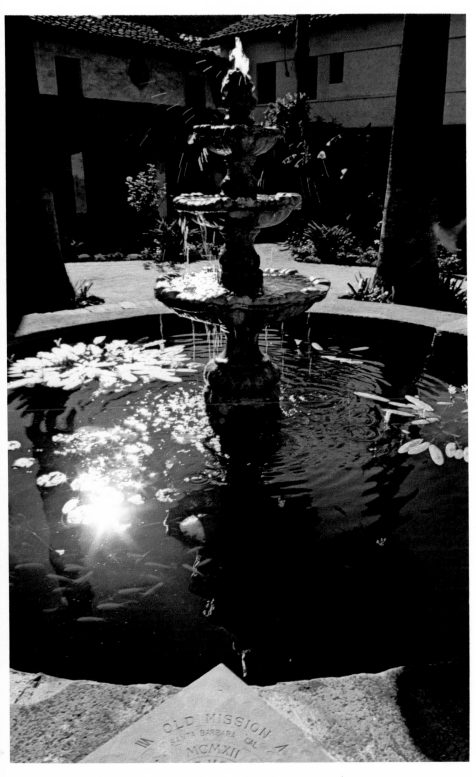

**QUEEN OF
ALL THE MISSIONS**
Unusual blending of Roman ornamentation with simplicity of mission style makes Santa Barbara Mission sparkle like a jewel. Tiered fountain is in patio enclosed by monastery buildings that once housed theological students for Franciscan priesthood.

For a different kind of RIDE get on the right TRACK

A foreign Chief of State visiting California expressed two burning desires. One was to visit Disneyland—which he couldn't, to his great disappointment. The other was to ride the train along the coast—which he did, to his great pleasure. Leaders have changed, but the incomparable rail trip remains a most delightful experience.

The long train glides down the fertile Salinas Valley, between fruit and nut orchards, through fields of artichokes, beans, grain. Skirting oil fields at San Ardo, it passes within sight of Mission San Miguel. At Pismo begins a glorious 113-mile run along the coastline with views of Point Conception and its lighthouse, of ominous missile gantries within Vandenberg Air Force Base, of immense cattle ranches. The landscape changes from jutting rocks and dry hillsides to fields of waving grasses and nodding wildflowers, from long beaches to sparkling ocean.

Though there may be faster modes of traveling, few are quite as satisfying.

"HERE SHE COMES!"
Headlights flashing and bells clanging, Amtrak's train rolls smoothly into Oakland depot in the day's early hours. Throughout the morning it runs the level length of Salinas Valley, then begins a winding climb up Cuesta Grade, plunging through tunnels and doubling back on itself.

"WATCH YOUR STEP!"
*Early-afternoon sun drenches San Luis
Obispo, left, where a few passengers detrain. A
couple of hours later comes the sparkling
Santa Barbara shore, with glimpses across
the channel of Santa Cruz Island, right. A brief
stop at Oxnard, another at Glendale, and, as
the sun drops low, the train arrives at
Los Angeles Union Station in time for supper.*

DRIVING
and dining
detour to
DENMARK

You couldn't call it a shortcut. Driving distance along this former stage route is about the same as it would be if you stayed on the freeway. In fact, the sidetrip could take from a couple of hours to a couple of days or longer. It all depends on how completely you surrender to the visual delights of San Marcos Pass and Santa Ynez Valley and the culinary temptations of Solvang, an Old World town founded by Danish Americans. Equally diverting are the frontier-style village of Santa Inez and time-mellowed Mission Santa Ines, fully restored and in daily use.

Whatever your ultimate destination and no matter how strongly sounds the siren call of the coast, this is an inland excursion not to be hurried.

SLOW WAY TO (OR FROM) SANTA BARBARA
Delightful detour bypasses a coastal corner of U.S. 101. Corrugated hills edging Lake Cachuma, right, are backed by rumpled ridges of San Rafael Range. Opposite: In the shadow of Santa Ynez Mountains, Solvang's spires and rooftops look like a scene from a Danish Christmas card.

The Channel Islands:
A Heritage
of Scenic Splendor

Birds, seals, and sea lions are the chief inhabitants of this unique place. For some species, these islands are the only sanctuary in this part of the world.

ROY MURPHY

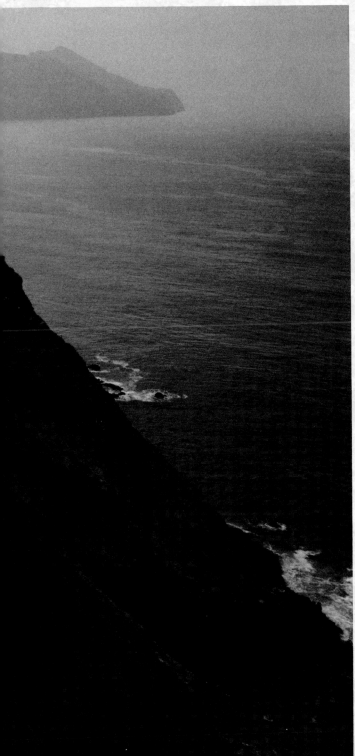

Thrusting out of the sea off the Southern California coast are eight craggy chunks of land collectively called the Channel Islands.

Most easily seen from Santa Barbara, privately owned Santa Cruz is largest in the chain. Stands of grasses, oaks, and pines also make it the greenest. Nearby is Santa Rosa Island, also privately owned.

Tiny San Nicolas was the lonely, 20-year abode of a solitary Chumash Indian woman, who was marooned when the rest of the island's population was evacuated by mission priests. Today, San Nicolas, San Miguel, and San Clemente are part of a U.S. Navy target range.

Nearest Los Angeles, Santa Catalina is world famous as a tourist destination (see page 233), even though the greater part of it is closed to the public.

Perhaps it says something about the priorities placed on natural resources that the two *smallest* islands—Anacapa and Santa Barbara—are set aside as a natural monument. Both are characterized by steep cliffs, dry hills, and little vegetation. Yet their austere charm—reminiscent of Scotland's outer Hebrides—makes a visit a calming kind of atavistic experience.

THREE ISLANDS IN ONE
At the eastern end of Santa Barbara Channel is a slender chain of three ragged bits of land, so closely joined as to form one: Anacapa Island (left). The dinosaurian spine of Anacapa's East Island stretches down from a plateau to a land link—uncovered at low tide—with its neighbors. The entire archipelago was once part of the mainland. Thousands of years ago, deformation of the earth's crust and a rise in sea level separated land masses from the continent, leaving a series of mountain tops poking above the ocean.

187

**SEA LIONS
AT SAN MIGUEL**
*Rookery for vast herds of sea lions,
San Miguel Island is also home for one of the
largest known colonies of elephant seals.
Otters and fur seals visit the island; pelicans,
cormorants, gulls, and foxes are permanent
residents. Portuguese explorer Juan Cabrillo
died here in 1543. Although he is reported
to be buried on San Miguel, his grave has
never been found.*

SUNSET AT SMUGGLER'S COVE

Glowing sky silhouettes a shoulder of Santa Cruz Island and isolates Anacapa on the horizon. Twenty-one miles long and five miles wide, Santa Cruz is largest of the offshore islands. It has protected coves, open meadows, and groves of pine and oak. At various times it has been a Mexican penal colony, a cattle ranch, and a sheep station.

BOB EVANS

THE LIGHTHOUSE THAT IS . . .
A CHURCH THAT ISN'T

Few permanent structures mar natural landscape of the monument. An exception is the lighthouse and accompanying Coast Guard station on Anacapa. Hallowed-looking building in the foreground is only a shell camouflaging the station's water supply. The storage tank proved too great a temptation for sharpshooting Mexican crewmen aboard fishing boats, was regularly peppered with rifle fire until it was disguised as a church.

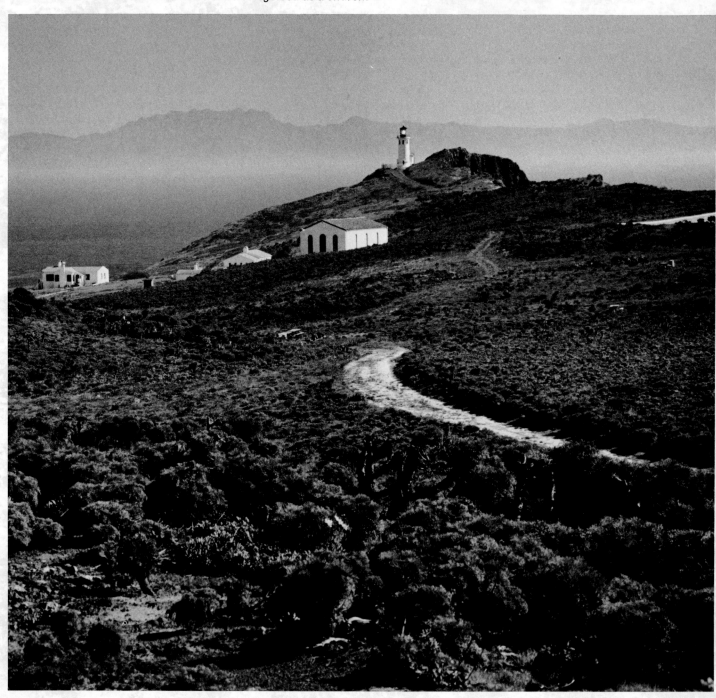

"There were more lobster and abalone than anyone ever wanted..."

Captain and owner of *Coral Sea,* an 85-foot charter cruiser, Glenn Miller has lived all of his life in Santa Barbara. Having operated boats for more than 20 years, he knows the Santa Barbara coast as do few other people.

"Over the years, I've seen a lot of pollution along the coast. The worst is from outfalls—sewage outfalls—that go right into the ocean. In front of Santa Barbara it used to be solid kelp from the wharf on down. Now there's none ... no kelp south of here. It's because of the outfall.

"Farther south, the Los Angeles outfall has really done a lot of damage. I've seen underwater pictures of the bottom, and there just isn't anything there except a kind of sludge. I remember years ago diving off Palos Verdes. There were plenty of lobsters and abalone. Now there are only sea urchins because they seem to congregate around outfalls. But the urchins eat kelp, so that kills it off.

"You see, kelp is a shelter for fish. And abalone live around it. But when there isn't any kelp, the marine life suffers. . . .

"The big oil spill here in 1969 made an awful mess. Oil all over the beaches, the water, the bottoms of boats. But, you know, except for killing some wildlife at the time—which certainly wasn't good—I haven't seen any real long-range effects.

"In 1974 I was out with some scientists from the State of California to see what damage had been done by the spill. We went to the islands—San Miguel, Santa Rosa, Anacapa, Santa Cruz —looking for damage, but we didn't find any. And this was five years after it happened.

"Historically, Santa Barbara Channel has had oil seepage. There's always been oil coming up out of the ground and the ocean. So it isn't anything new around here. At my house in Goleta, I can smell oil on a warm day from around Coal Oil Point. The stuff that seeps up isn't usable. It's sticky, like tar or asphalt. It sure makes a mess on a boat hull.

"It's when there's a big blowout or a spill that the papers pick it up and the news is on everybody's mind. The oil companies are supercareful about spills nowadays. . . .

"The Channel Islands are the most interesting part of this coast. San Miguel is about 30 miles off Point Conception. It's a sea lion rookery. There are thousands of them.

"A man named Herbert Lester lived there with his family a long time ago. His wife was a teacher, so their daughter had schooling right at home. When World War II started, the government told Lester he had to leave. I guess he didn't want to go because he went out and shot himself. He's buried on the island.

"San Nicolas is a Navy island. There's a lot of abalone there because it's so remote. But Anacapa and Santa Cruz and Santa Rosa are pretty well picked over. The lobsters are really going downhill. Not too long ago, there were more lobsters and abalone than anyone ever wanted."

OIL
is a slippery issue along the
SOUTHERN
shore

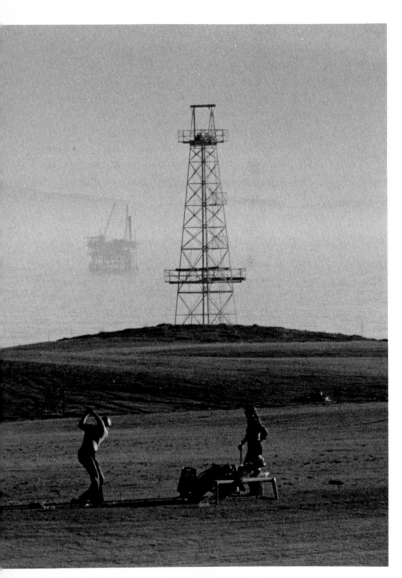

Until recent years, Santa Barbara lived more or less harmoniously with petroleum. Familiar with the thick, black stuff that seeped out of the ground, coastal Indians used it to seal their canoes. English seafarer George Vancouver—visiting the area in the late 1700s—mentioned the channel being covered with a sticky substance. As early as 1896, a well was sunk in the channel at Santa Barbara, and in the 1920s drilling began in the Elwood Field, near Goleta.

In the mid-1960s, exploratory drilling offshore—triggered by state and federal lease sales—created an increased awareness of what could be done to the natural landscape by pollution. Citizens and concerned politicians urged a moderate pace, to give at least enough time for further studies, but drilling went on at an increasing rate.

Then on January 28, 1969, oil became a word heard around the world: a blowout occurred in the channel. Although contained at the drilling platform, millions of gallons of black muck, forced out of fissures on the sea floor, washed ashore.

Though the popular villain, the oil industry was quick to respond, paying heavily in hours and dollars to clean up the mess. Equally quick was the hue and cry raised by Santa Barbarans. Today there exists a standoff between Santa Barbara and those who would drill holes anywhere in the vicinity.

A LONG DRIVE

In the heat of the game, a golfer ignores oil platforms, even though one seems to be a greens' marker. Exploration of potential deposits may necessitate boring holes as much as two miles deep through varied strata, right. Because of coastal slope, offshore sites sometimes require less drilling to reach layers of spongy rock that hold oil, but supporting the ocean-anchored operation calls for more massive rigs.

OCEANIC ISLAND *Looking as if thrust up out of the sea, an offshore drilling platform looms against the horizon. Supported on a forest of steel pilings, such platforms are supplied with power and water from shore, or use self-contained power sources.*

The town's real title is San Buenaventura, after the patron saint whose name was bestowed on the last mission founded by Father Junipero Serra. But in 1891 the name of the farming center was abbreviated because it was too long and too difficult to pronounce and because mail was finding its way to San Bernardino. Though the name is smaller than it once was, the town is not. Ventura, Oxnard, and Port Hueneme—once separated by acres of agricultural land—are now blending into one coastal metropolis. Crowded out by ever-new industry, citrus, celery, tomatoes, strawberries, and avocados are becoming less apparent near the shore.

SAILING
Its canvas holding a breeze, a sloop "stands" out of Ventura Marina, while power cruisers lie snug at their slips. Marina is a casting-off point for voyages to Channel Islands National Monument.

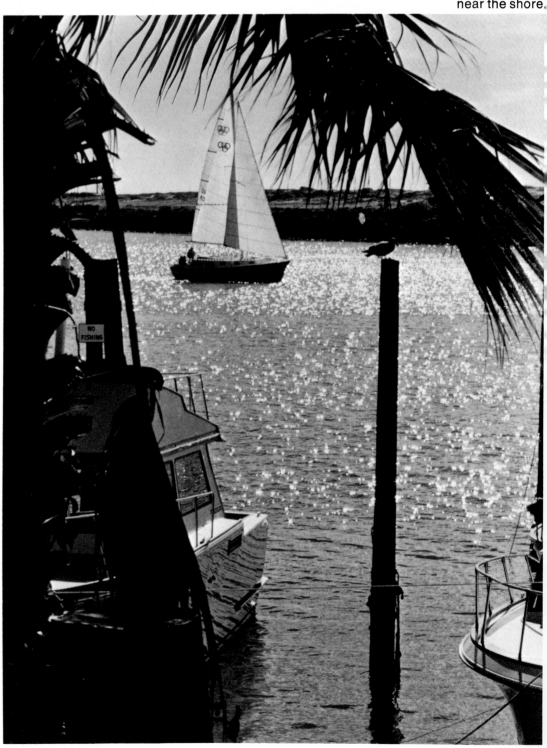

Ventura's
PLEASURES afloat,
TREASURES ashore

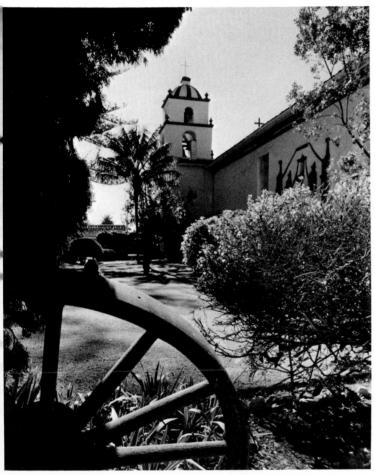

SURVIVING
*Mission San Buenaventura—built in 1782—
has outlived fire, earthquake, Indian
unrest, threat of pirate attack, and a craze
for modernization. Its museum houses
the only wooden bells ever used in a
California mission.*

SUNNING
*Tiny tummies take kindly to salt air and warm
sun at State Beach. Despite the presence
of numerous commercial developments
that seem to lunge out of the sand, the
Ventura waterfront is a most enjoyable
shoreside recreational area.*

SIGHTSEEING
sidetrip to
SHANGRI-LA

Destination: Shangri-La, legendary paradise, in actuality a magnificent vista used in the 1930s film, "Lost Horizon." Round-trip distance from Santa Barbara: Approximately 100 miles. Leisurely driving time: 3 or 4 hours. Highlights of the trip: Avocado orchards and cutflower fields east of Santa Barbara . . . views to the southwest of the channel islands . . . boating, picnicking at Lake Casitas . . . early Spanish day atmosphere of Ojai village . . . vistas of rugged mountain terrain . . . sweeping views of Shangri-La (the Ojai Valley) . . . oil museum at Santa Paula . . . citrus orchards and ranches east of Ventura . . . San Buenaventura Mission at Ventura. Tip: Instead of taking U.S. 101 back to Santa Barbara, turn off at Emma Wood State Beach, just north of Ventura, and drive along the old coast highway.

ALONG THE WAY . . .
Favorite spot for those who enjoy boating, camping, or fishing, Lake Casitas Recreation Area snuggles in lower valley west of town of Ojai. Rolling hills and soft meadows dominate the landscape.

. . . AND THE PLACE TO STAY

Ojai Valley panorama from Dennison Grade reveals a tidy bottomland dotted with orchards and ranches. Sheltered against fog, smog, and wind, the area attracts many visitors who, charmed by the easy-going atmosphere and blossom-scented air, return to take up permanent residence.

A gull skims along a curling wave, its wingtip almost touching the crest, its body motionless, its face impassive. Too sleepy to do more than grumble, a sea lion lazing on a rock watches the bird soar past. Low and unambitious, the surf washes softly over the sand, stretching thin like a wakening cat, before sliding again into the sea. Thin fog creeps back and forth, trying to decide whether to lie over the water or infiltrate farther inland. A pale blob in the haze, a fishing boat slips by, the sound of its engine a muffled chug-chug-chug. When the world closes in on a person, the beach is an open place, a place to be alone.

A SOLITARY SILENCE
There is a touch of surrealism in a girl meditating in a sea of footprints—a feeling that everyone else on earth has vanished, leaving a oneness of sky, sea, and self. The ocean-quiet invitation to ramble is accepted by a jaunty lad, who traipses happily along the shore, right.

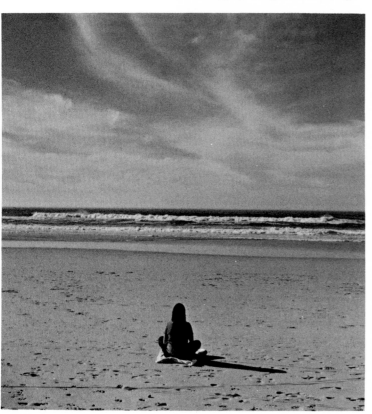

BOB ISAACS

A BEACH is
a place
to be ALONE

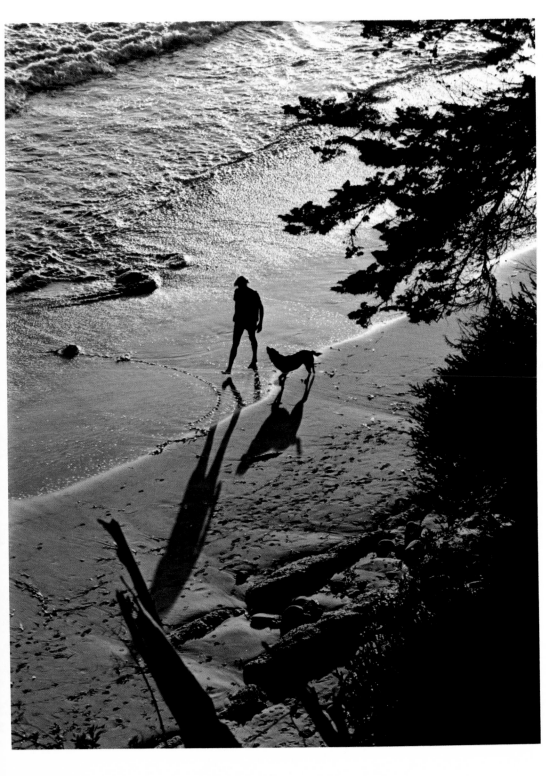

**A SOCIETY
OF SOLITUDE**
*Alone but not lonely, a
stroller and his playful but
silent companion idle
their way down a wave-
washed beach.*

New developments in the ROCKET'S red glare

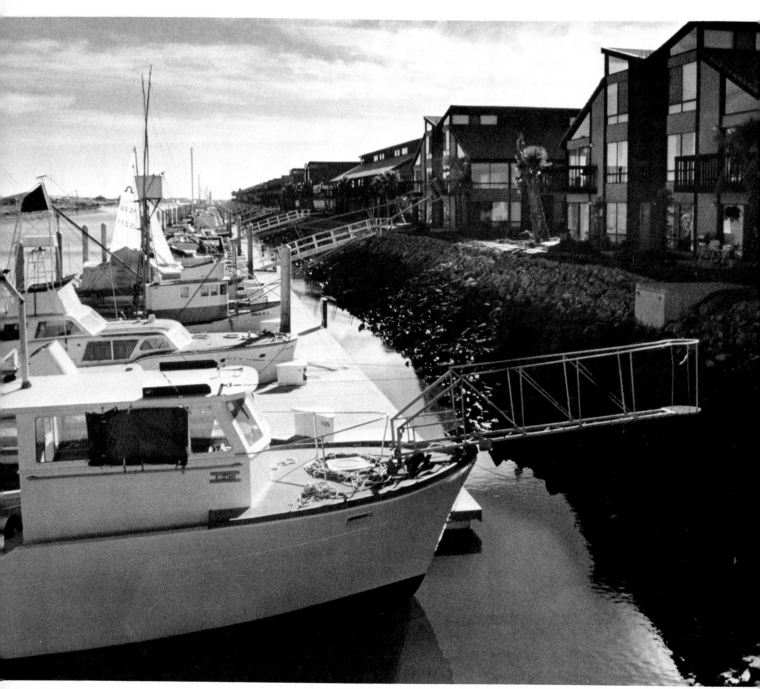

YOU CAN'T LIVE
MUCH CLOSER TO THE WATER

Almost afloat, blocks of high-intensity dwellings back up to floating docks, easing the transition from living room to launch. For the weekend sailor, increased leisure time enhances the appeal of "waterfront apartments," such as these at Oxnard.

In 1512 Spanish explorer Juan Cabrillo rhapsodically described the area as a "land of everlasting summers" and noted that some 50,000 Chumash Indians were enjoying the mild climate. Sun and fertile soil led to the establishment—almost 400 years later—of a sugar beet processing center that was eventually called Oxnard. The town and its surroundings have expanded in all directions, including up. Where beet sprouts once reached toward the sun, experimental missiles now soar skyward, guided by the U.S. Navy at Point Mugu. Where sand and soil lay undisturbed except by a sea breeze, apartments, ocean front homes, and beach cottages rise.

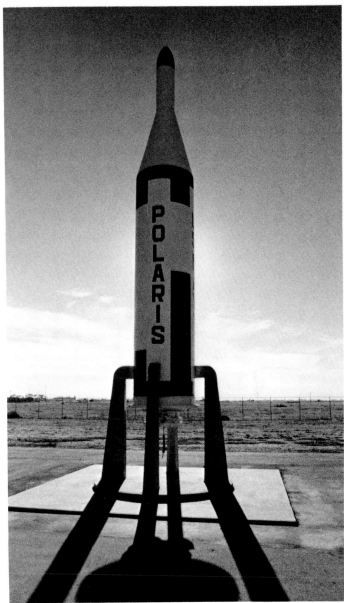

CELERY AND SIDEWINDERS

Once a rich agricultural area, the coastal strip behind Oxnard is losing ground to pressures for commercial development. At Point Mugu—where the U.S. Navy hurls its missiles out over the Pacific— Polaris, Bullpup, and other exotically christened rockets tower at an informative roadside display.

Seaward Los

Along the densely populated seaward side of Los Angeles, a few natural wetlands, quiet estuaries, undeveloped mountain tops, and unbuilt-upon hillsides contrast dramatically with the region's urban character. Viewing the coast by land, from sea, or from air, a traveler is vividly aware of miles of developed waterfront, only occasionally relieved by patches of natural preserves.

Intensified land use along this coastal strip has resulted in a hectic mix of power plants, petroleum refineries, oil wells, and various industrial activities. This is the land of high-rise. This is the coast of condominiums, commercial development, and controlled recreation.

Fronting on upper Santa Monica Bay are several broad strands. Access to these beaches —as well as to the entire coastal stretch from Point Dume to Santa Monica—is provided by the Pacific Coast Highway, a sea-skirting route whose capacity is exceeded on any sunny weekend. Venice—a former dream city of canals, gondolas, and amusement halls—jealously withholds from developers its strip of fine beach and fishing pier.

More miles of "perfect" sand reach along the lower rim of Santa Monica Bay from El Segundo to Redondo Beach, abutting the Palos Verdes Peninsula, an east-west belt of natural landscape.

Lower Newport Bay provides a water-oriented life style, and the Laguna shore has a lively, Rivieralike quality. By contrast, San Clemente, Dana Point, and Capistrano Beach are quiet settlements.

Angeles

Work, a Passion for Play

Here build your homes for good,
　establish here, these areas entire,
　lands of the Western shore . . .
At last the New arriving, assuming,
　taking possession,
A swarming and busy race settling
　and organizing everywhere. . . .
　　　　　　—Walt Whitman

Point Dume

Santa Monica

Los Angeles

Palos Verdes Point

Long Beach

Santa Catalina Island

San Clemente Island

Laguna Beach

San Juan Capistrano

101

405

1

1

405

5

5

14

N

LIVING CLOSE
to the water's edge

Statistics hint broadly at California's love affair with the sea: 85 percent of the population lives within 30 miles of the ocean. Nowhere is this liaison more evident than on the southern coast. From the lower edge of the Santa Monica Mountains to Newport Bay, civilization marches up to and sometimes over the waterfront. Competition is fierce for waterfront real estate in the densely settled, land-hungry southland. In some places beach dwellers have partitioned off stretches of sand in front of their homes. "We don't want everyone tramping through our front yard," is their posture. From the homeowner's point of view, the practice may be understandable—but it is illegal. Only a law saved public access to the narrow strip of sand along the Malibu shore. To the nearby population, the shore is important as a major recreation area. Every precious inch is used.

SHORELINE AT MALIBU
Long and level stretches the beachfront, but the inviting strand is only marginally accessible except to beach residents. For several miles along the ocean edge, a phalanx of stilt-supported homes visually and physically separates the Pacific Coast Highway from its namesake.

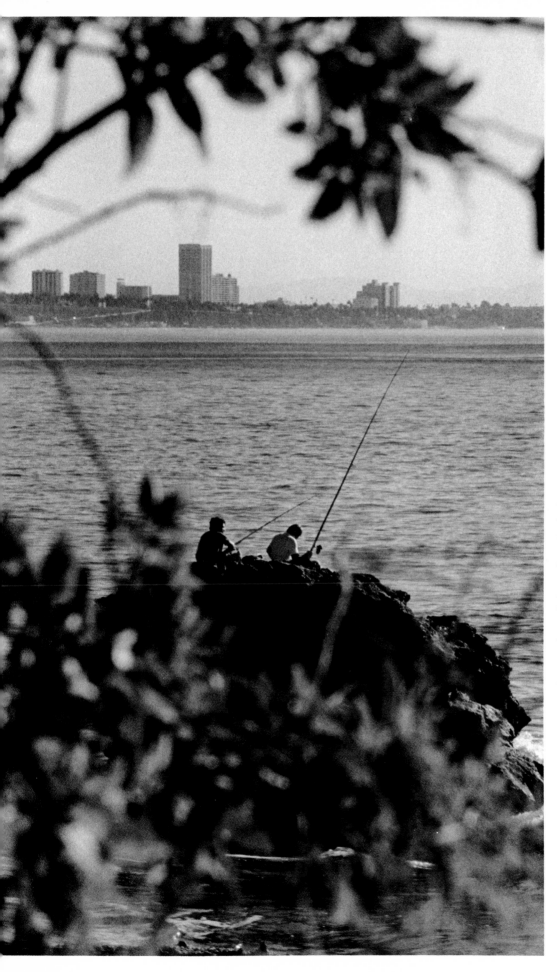

**SKYLINE AT
SANTA MONICA**
Rock fishermen take their
ease while trying their luck
near Las Tunas State
Beach. Situated on high
bluffs overlooking the
ocean, the city of Santa
Monica has come close to
losing its touch with
the sea. In the early 1970s,
a startling proposal was
made to slice Santa Monica
Bay with an offshore
causeway topped with
high-rise apartments and a
freeway. The scheme
was shelved.

...CLOSE TO THE WATER

J.R. EYERMAN

SOME OF THE MOST INTENSIVELY DEVELOPED SHORE IN THE WORLD Tying together one town after another, the Los Angeles shoreline threads its narrow way along natural and manmade landscape. Largely undeveloped in the north (bottom of photo), the Santa Monica Mountains grade down to the popular Los Angeles Plain, and open seaside becomes increasingly close-packed as it skirts Santa Monica Bay southward (top of photo).

COMPETITION ON THE COAST
In some places the southland's shore is so heavily settled that water's edge becomes difficult to trace. At Redondo Beach King Harbor, left, a large marina appears to be tangling masts with towers of a waterfront apartment complex and smokestacks of a closely sited power plant. Below: Broad Torrance Beach sands give way to layers of homes stairstepping up the northern slope of Palos Verdes peninsula.

Boomers and breakers, or the art of HANGING TEN

CAREFUL BEGINNING
Not yet a novice, a cautious tyro braces against the backwash, clutching his belly board. He's enthralled by antics of experts riding big combers farther out. Inland, an agile enthusiast manages to balance board, wetsuit, and himself all on two wheels.

In search of a long ride on the perfect wave, surfing aficionados flock to Southern California's shore, where the gently sloping sea floor manufactures just the right kind of wave, called "the spilling breaker."

Surfing first came to California from Hawaii in 1907, when the champion of Waikiki gave exhibitions at Redondo Beach. But apparently the sport didn't catch on until Hollywood imported Duke Kahanamoku to appear in films of the 1920s. In a matter of weeks, dozens of would-be imitators with backyard versions of his massive board appeared on the beach. Boards are incomparably better now (most of them are fiberglass), but because of their efficient shapes, challenging waves are harder to find.

FLYING FINISH
Hot-dogging it all the way to the beach, a single-minded surfer is oblivious to high-flying board of a wipeout victim who has been totally consumed in the sport.

Forty miles of SAND, forty million SUN seekers

What can you do on a Los Angeles beach? An urban-weary population in search of renewal finds both action and leisure there the year around. One estimate places the number of visitors at 40 million annually— a lot of square footage of sunburned skin. The beaches are family fun, havens for the young, an athlete's delight, and, in winter, a more or less solitary strand for quiet strollers. But it's the summer that finds the public beaches paved with languid bodies. The sea of humanity spills into the surf where the more restless have devised endless ways to play in the waves. For the die-hard beacher, activity continues late into the evening, with picnic fires blazing in concrete rings.

*SOUTHLANDERS REALLY
USE THEIR SHORE*
*Most popular sector of the Los Angeles
Coast—at least from the standpoint of
numbers—is Santa Monica Beach State
Park. Thousands of sun-worshipping surfers,
swimmers, and picnickers are drawn to the
beach on a bright summer day.*

SUN FUN IS EASILY FOUND
Intense concentration furrows faces of
volleyball players. Most popular beach
sport, volleyball brings a dedicated breed to
the shore shortly after sunrise and holds
them there until dusk. Almost anywhere, one
who loves the beach will find the perfect
combination of sun and sea, above.

TIDES
are giant waves

The tug of moon and sun on the sea creates a halfway world. In the narrow ribbon between high and low tides, a diverse array of creatures lives a rigorous in-and-out-again existence. Barnacles and periwinkle snails need only intermittent splashes; varieties of anemones and stars are completely covered except during the lowest tides. The species living in tidepools—the harshest environment—fall somewhere in between in their need for water.

Buffeting waves, evaporation, and fresh water brought by heavy rains are a few of the threats to life in this mid-zone. But the greatest of dangers is man's inquisitiveness and acquisitiveness. Every rock shields a rich variety of living things, and collectors who move stones or take home specimens are hastening the demise of intertidal life. The best policy is a self-imposed one: look and enjoy, but don't remove.

ONE ON THE ROCKS
Stepping from one slippery spot to another, an intrepid explorer scans rocky inlets exposed during lowest tide of the year. Canvas sneakers are ideal footwear for such excursions; they grip well and dry readily after a sloshing.

THREE IN THE SHALLOWS

Dwelling in pools that drain to dampness on ebb tide is a varied community of highly adapted animals. Starfish (top) wrap sucker-lined arms around clams and force the shellfish open by a constant pull, then extend their stomach into shell to digest its contents. Tentacles of flowerlike anemones (center) capture food that drifts or swims by, contracting when danger threatens. Urchins (bottom) feed on small organisms on sea floor and move by "walking" their spines.

*A CRAB IN THE HAND IS
WORTH TWO IN THE SAND*
*Though not hefty enough to
give a sizeable nip on a
finger, sand crabs can
startle an unsuspecting
sand castle engineer by
suddenly scuttling over a
digging hand. Lying just
below the surface of the
wave-washed beach
with their eye stalks thrust
above into the water, sand
crabs wait patiently for tides
and currents to bring food
particles their way.*

BOB ISAACS

TURNING OF THE TIDES

Regular rise and fall of ocean waters is caused by gravitational pull of moon and by centrifugal force of spinning earth. When earth, moon, and sun are in a line—as at new and full moon—force is greatest, causing spring tides (spring refers not to season but to "springing up" of the waters). Neap (or nipped) tides occur when sun and moon exert force at right angles to one another.

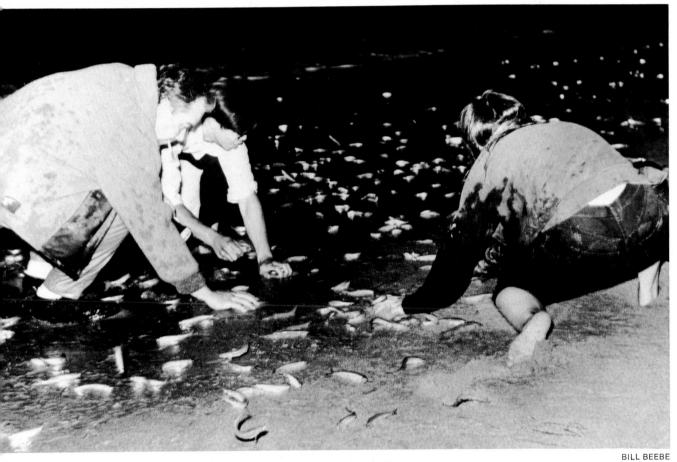

BILL BEEBE

YES, VIRGINIA, THERE REALLY IS A GRUNION   It sounds like a gag, but in Southern California, stalking fish with a flashlight is a pastime rather than a practical joke. During highest spring and summer tides, silver sided *Leuresthes tenuis (commonly known as grunion)* wriggle ashore to spawn. Fertilized eggs remain above subsequent low tides until uncovered by the next high tide, when the hatchlings wash out to deeper waters.

Marina Del Rey modestly calls itself the world's largest boat garage, and no one has challenged the claim. The manmade harbor comfortably accommodates up to 10,000 pleasure craft that sometimes all seem to be coming and going at once. Dredged from a salt water lagoon that was once popular with duck hunters, the marina sits behind the dune barrier that separates it from Santa Monica Bay. It is maintained for public use by Los Angeles County, but private developers have transformed its shores into a Venice-like city by the sea. Shops, office buildings, marine services, and luxury condominiums only a few steps from the slips bring the stylish world to the boat owner's gangplank.

ANIMATION ON ALL LEVELS
As modern as today, a pair of sloops tack spiritedly down the channel, slipping past old schooners and a square-rigged bark dozing at Fisherman's Village moorings, right. Below: Small craft fuss around a multi-lane launch ramp, just a stone's throw from a soaring multi-story office building.

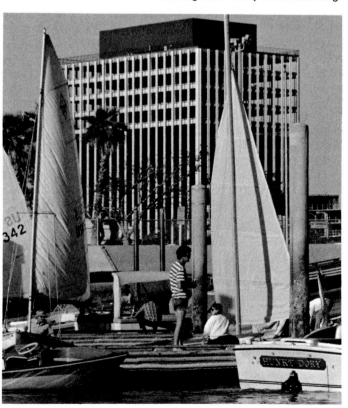

Luxury, LEISURE, and a watery way of LIFE

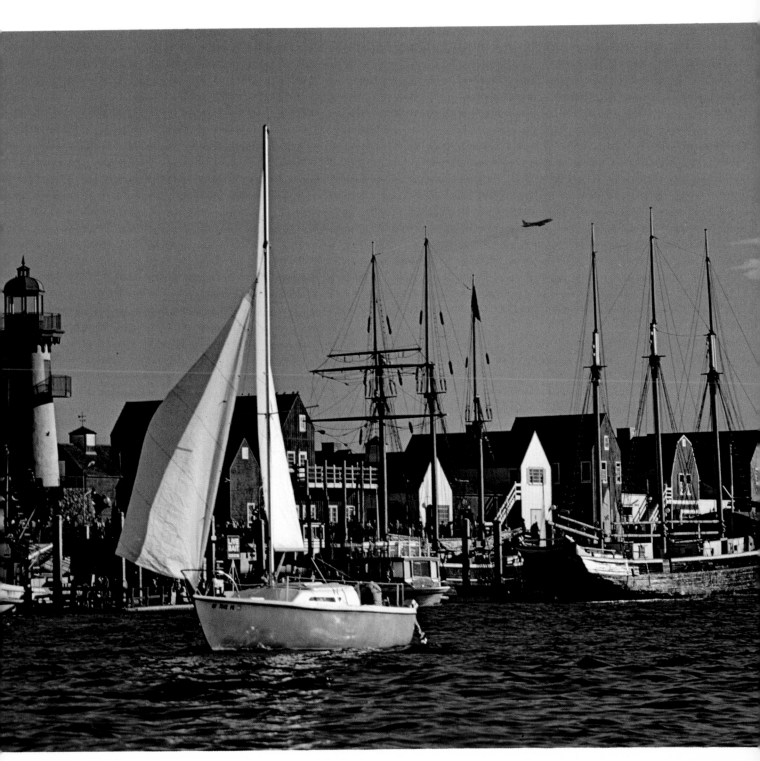

Palos Verdes: Shoreside Refuge for the Urban-Weary

The City of the Angels reaches out for land, but in one coastal area the relentless march of development has been held back by a buffer of natural beauty.

The peninsula of Palos Verdes, which means "green trees," is the last vestige of the vast Rancho de Palo Verdes that remains true to its name. Once an island, now an arm of land that thrusts its rocky fist between the flat sand beaches of Santa Monica Bay and the harbor of Los Angeles, Palos Verdes has been protected by its residents from the dense development that pushes hard against its inland flank. Some areas are officially preserved as parks and state beaches, but many of the coves and bights below steep bluffs remain unspoiled because of their relative isolation.

The truce with civilization is not altogether perfect. Spectacular scenery of the cliff-top drive and the educational entertainment offered by Marineland of the Pacific draw thousands of visitors to the peninsula, a fact sometimes decried by its permanent population. Offshore, a sewer outfall has destroyed the once-giant kelp beds. Nonetheless, residents still regard their wooded hills as the only sanctuary of natural seaside beauty that has not succumbed to the sprawling city.

THIS IS A LIVING MARINE PRESERVE PLEASE HELP US PRESERVE IT
- Taking of most tidal invertebrates forbidden (C.A.C. Title 14 Sec. 51).
- Always return tide pool animals to their original habitat after studying them.
- Please take nothing from the preserve. All animals, algae, shells, etc., should be left in place.
- Return rocks to their original position after you have finished observing their undersides.
- Carry no glass or other containers with you into the marine preserve.
- Practice conservation—it is a good habit to acquire. Carry all of your litter back to a trash can.

Palos Verdes Estates Shoreline Preserve

LEAVING THE LANDSCAPE ALONE
Facing page: Brush and free-growing grasses blend red tile roofs and whitewashed walls of a Mediterranean-style structure fronting on Malaga Cove. Above: A solitary figure finds serenity in contemplating the open sea from a grassy knoll. Nearby sign is a gentle reminder that shoreline is a protected area.

SEAWARD, AN OCEAN-GOING OUTLOOK

Getting to the waters that lap the Palos Verdes shore sometimes requires the agility of a mountain goat, but determined skindivers and surfers make it down to Lunada Bay, above, even carrying a full complement of equipment. Glass walls and redwood beams of Wayfarer's Chapel, right, harmonize perfectly with setting of cedar, pine, and eucalyptus. The peaceful place of meditation looks over busy Marineland of the Pacific to the ocean.

INLAND, A PARCEL OF THE NATURAL WORLD Early-morning sun streaming through a thin haze brightens commuters' route as they roll downhill, in no hurry to join with hustle and noise of another working day. Claims one Palos Verdes resident: "There may be a great many homes up here, but this is the only place around Los Angeles where there's some natural world left near the ocean . . . I hate to leave it even for a few hours."

With strollers or sitters,
PUBLIC PIERS
are popular

Public piers abound in the southland. More than in the north, they jut from almost every beach as one way of extending well-used recreation areas. Those who most value these boardwalks on stilts are either confirmed anglers or chronic strollers. The former aren't fussy about niceties. Their contentment lies in having enough water to wet a line. The latter take their pleasure in sniffing the sea air, browsing among whatever concessions may be available (though even these are secondary to sunshine and salt breezes), and occasionally passing the time of day with others of their ilk—including fishermen.

SOMETHING FOR EVERYBODY
Last light of day is shared by steadfast anglers and never-say-die surfers at Manhattan Beach, above. Mutual respect prevents encounters between lines and boards. A strollers' utopia, shops and restaurants of lively Redondo State Beach spread along the shore, covering not one but two popular piers, right.

JUST TAKING IT EASY
Day after day, addicts of pier fishing return to the same spot, ever cheerful, ever contented, caring little if they catch anything. "Sometimes I don't even bait the hook ..." confided a Newport angler, below. "I get my fun just sitting here." Coin-operated binoculars regard such frivolities with drooping eyes.

OUTWARD BOUND
Riding high in the water, a tanker rounds the bluff of Point Vicente and heads northward. Despite lonely look of the scene, shipping lanes in and out of Los Angeles Harbor are among world's busiest, and traffic day or night is heavy.

TWIN PORTS that are tops in TONNAGE

The quantitative data of Los Angeles Harbor are impressive. Nine miles of breakwater embrace San Pedro Bay, cordoning off the colossal complex of the Ports of Los Angeles and Long Beach. Fifty miles of waterfront are a panorama of clamorous, sweating, perpetual motion. In 1973-74 thousands of cargo ships loaded and unloaded nearly 30 million tons of goods valued at $5½ billion. Nine shipyards build and maintain craft of every kind, from outboard motorboats to supertankers. Fishing boats market their catch to the seafood canning industry, which is also based here. All this, plus a waterfront recreation area and the mammoth *Queen Mary*—now a floating museum and hotel—compete for one's attention almost as fiercely as the two ports vie with each other.

THE INNER PASSAGE
Towering tall even when viewed from San Pedro across the main channel, cargo cranes on Terminal Island, left, are used in handling seagoing container shipments. Of Bombay registry, Vishva Nayak *uses her own booms to offload an exotic lading of rubber, carpets, and preserved fish. Bulbous affair at ship's bow helps prevent rolling in rough seas and subsequent damage to goods.*

...PORT OF LOS ANGELES

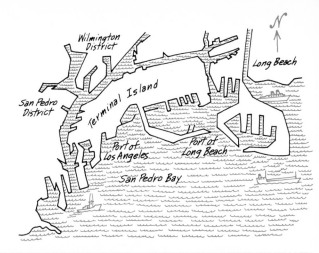

IT'S A WIDE, WATERY WORLD . . .
Located at western end of San Pedro Bay,
the vast Port of Los Angeles comprises over
7,000 acres of land and water. In photo, a
containerized ship heads up the main
channel, passing quarantine station at the
tip of Terminal Island.

PORT OF LOS ANGELES

. . . AN ENERGETIC, INDUSTRIAL WORLD

Riding low in the water, a trawler hustles to dock, above, while crewmen secure the working gear and make ready for offloading operation. High and dry freighter in background is drydocked for repairs. Left: Overflowing boxes and bulging purse nets are winched out of Betty Ann's hold, emptying a part of her 20-ton catch of squid.

STEP INTO ANOTHER ERA
Two million visitors a year browse through the quaint shops and tempting eating places that make up an imaginative recreation area along the San Pedro waterfront. Ports o' Call is a replica of a California seacoast town of the 19th century, complete with non-California cobblestones. At adjoining Whaler's Wharf Village, wooden docks help recreate the New Bedford whaling era.

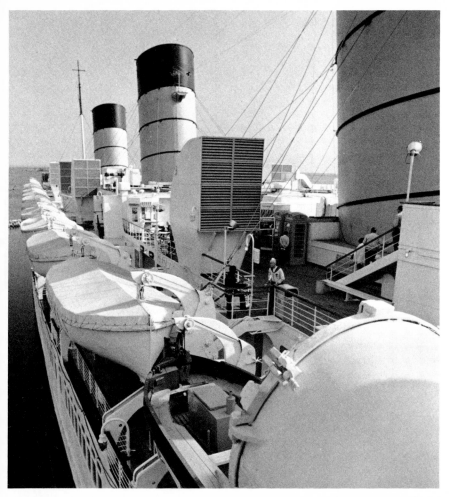

TAKE A TRIP TO SEE
Moored permanently at the end of the Long Beach Freeway—after being retired from active service in 1967—the stately Queen Mary offers everyone an opportunity to step aboard a luxury liner. The monarch of the Atlantic is now an enormous maritime museum that includes Jacques Cousteau's Living Sea exhibit. Below: "Passengers" inspect a gleaming array of controls on ship's bridge.

Discovering
the SQUISHY world
of the MARSHLAND

Marshes, lagoons, sloughs, and estuaries hide great wealth in their muddy expanses. Their waters serve as a spawning ground and nursery for large numbers of ocean fish, shellfish, crabs, and shrimp. Their bogs harbor thousands of migratory birds. Their plants manufacture large quantities of oxygen. Too often oblivious to such treasures, man seeks to exploit the "unproductive" space of wetlands—to fill them, dam them, dredge them, drain them.

Only 125,000 acres of wetlands remain in the state, down over half from the turn of the century. Along the north coast, many marshes exist virtually in a primitive condition simply because of a relatively light population. In Southern California, though, where the pressure to claim new land is greater, 75 percent of the wetlands have been destroyed. The trend has been slowed but not halted. Thanks to increasing public awareness, several coastal wetlands have been saved from subdivision by being made state wildlife preserves.

UNDERSTANDING
AN ESTUARY
Except for indomitable fishermen, few people love wetlands at first sight. The somber beauty takes time to appreciate, and the soggy underfooting does little in the way of extending an invitation. However, when estuaries, marshes, and tidal flats are viewed as a living resource, they are seen in a different light.

HARVEY HALVORSON

230

WETLANDS ARE NOT WASTELANDS

Most coastal estuaries go unnoticed by the traveler who is bent on getting somewhere and who sees them as unfit for human habitation. But those backwaters that have escaped silting and road fill are incredibly productive places that are home to innumerable creatures of sea and land.

Night heron   IAN TAIT

Blue heron   TOM MYERS

Belted kingfisher   TOM MYERS

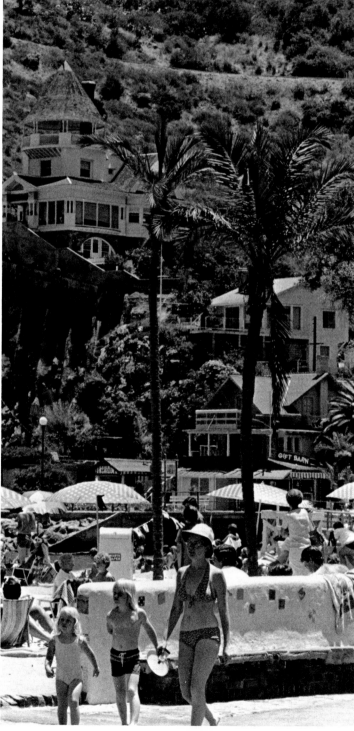

THE BIG, WHITE STEAMER
It's a twenty-minute flight by amphibious
airliner or a two-hour sea voyage by steamer,
above. Backpackers have arranged for an
overnight stay inland; casual sun
worshippers, right, spend their day strolling
the streets of bustling Avalon.

On a clear day you can see CATALINA

"Santa Catalina," crooned an old song, "island of romance." On a summer weekend, the island of romance is more like Coney Island. At least the square-mile town of Avalon seems that way as a steady procession of boats and seaplanes deposits yet another load of fun seekers. Once a sightseer is there, the biggest problem is deciding what to do.

Water lovers are enticed by swimming, boating, snorkeling, and scuba diving. Sport fishing craft are waiting for those who want to take up the challenge of topping tuna, marlin, and broadbill swordfish records. For passengers aboard the great, glass-bottomed sidewheelers, the unusually clear ocean allows detailed views of underwater gardens and intriguing sea creatures.

Landlubbers can turn away from the buzzing waterfront and tour part of the island's interior. Behind Avalon lie 75 square miles of primitive back country, the private estate of the Wrigley family. A few roads loop the low, brown mountains; several riding and hiking trails drift off into the chaparral-covered slopes and canyons. Because the island has been dedicated as a closed wilderness, only some wild goats and pigs and a herd of buffalo left behind by a Hollywood film-making crew can roam freely without permission.

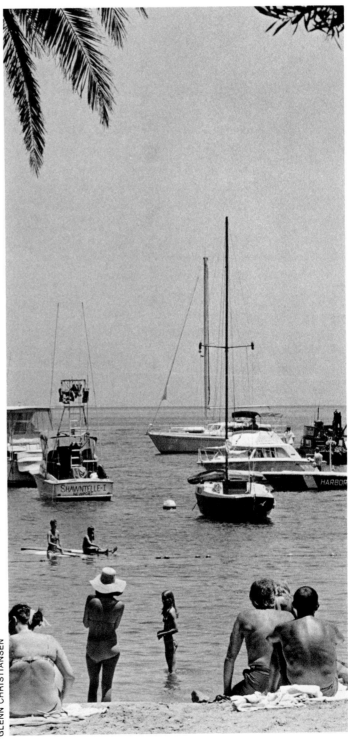

THE BIG, BUSY BAY
Though it's a "tropical" island—complete with waving palms and blue lagoons—Catalina is hardly a secret hideaway, especially during the busy summer sessions. Private craft jam Avalon Bay in such numbers that harbor patrol boats must do traffic duty.

GLENN CHRISTIANSEN

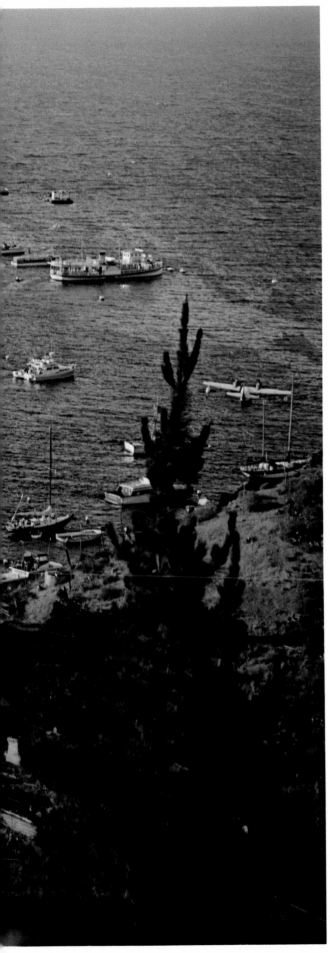

**"IN ALL THE WORLD,
NO TRIP LIKE THIS"**

Passengers debark on Avalon dock from one amphibian plane, far left, as another hustles seaward for takeoff. Luxury yachts democratically bob at anchor next to outboards, and at bay entrance a glass bottom sidewheeler settles down for the night like a mother hen. Harbor view looking north to Casino (actually a ballroom and movie theatre) has changed little in 50 years.

"AT LEAST THEY'RE QUIET"
"...and if one starts to squeak, they just put
a little oil on it...we've got plenty of that
around here." Huntington Beach residents
are not perturbed at having an idiotically
nodding pump for a next-door neighbor,
above. But petroleum can be annoying to
beach users when it occasionally appears
in sticky blobs that cling to bare feet.

LIVING in the considerable presence of PETROLEUM

The presence of oil is a foregone conclusion in Los Angeles. It has been since 1892, when wildcat prospector Edward L. Doheny tapped a bonanza that had derricks springing up from the downtown district to the surrounding hills. There are now over 9,000 producing wells in Los Angeles and Orange Counties.

In some places the industry has attempted to improve the appearance of the rigs by disguising drilling towers as office and apartment buildings, by hiding pumps underground, or by softening installations with landscaping. But because there are too many to camouflage, platforms and pumps sprout incongruously along beaches, in residential backyards, and in shopping districts. People have simply become accustomed to the sight—and to the pervasive smell on warm days. "That," said one Angeleno, sniffing the air, "smells like money."

ISLAND OF OIL
"Site unseen" oil platforms in Long Beach Harbor, below, are disguised as inhabited islands, complete with high-rise buildings covering drilling towers. From north of Seal Beach to south of Huntington Beach, the coast highway threads through an eerie thicket of stark derricks and uncovered pumps, above.

Helping hands haul the flat-bottomed boats from the surf, and umbrellas bloom as the beach by the Newport Pier becomes an open-air fish market. Its proprietors are the masters of a dozen 15½-foot dories, the last fishing fleet of its kind in the United States. Fishing methods were adopted from the New England cod fisherman. Early morning finds the doryman 10 miles off the coast, deftly paying out trawl lines coiled in a wooden keg and praying for luck. Then, laboriously cranking on a hand winch, he hauls his catch aboard and heads for home. As buyers eagerly call orders for the favored red rockfish or an occasional lobster, the job of baiting hooks for the next day's run begins again.

FRESH FILLETS TO ORDER
The day's fishing is completed by late morning, and market is set up at the foot of Newport Pier. A plank cutting board across a boat's stern, a scale hung on an oar stuck in the sand, and business begins as the doryman cleans and cuts up the catch any way the customer wants.

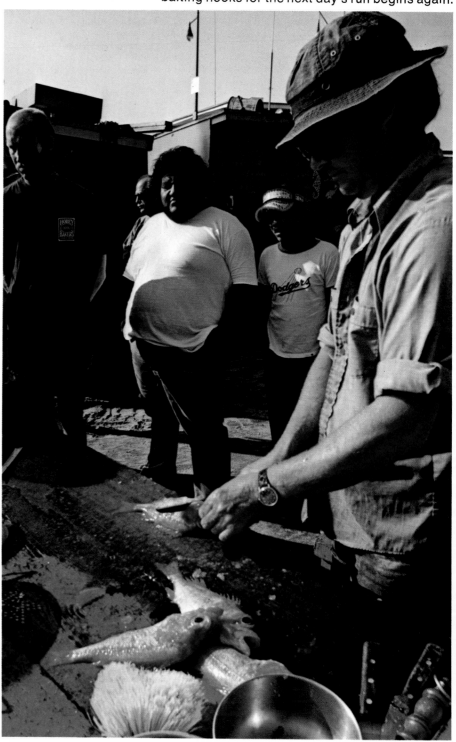

NEW ENGLAND
in **Newport, home of the**
DORY **fishermen**

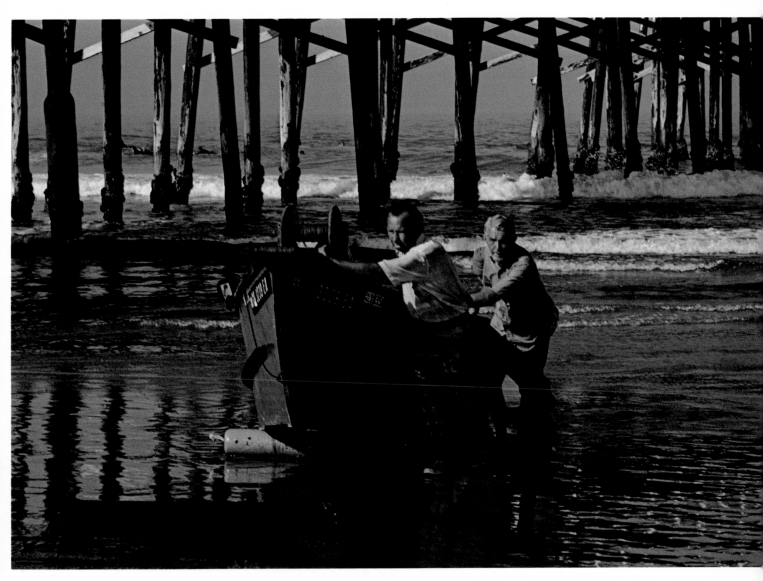

A HARD DAY
IS HALF-DONE   *An outboard motor drives the Gloucester dories through the surf, and muscle power pushes them over rollers to the marketplace far up the beach. The first boat of the day to pass the far end of Newport Pier traditionally gets "first spot," a favored selling site nearest the street.*

Pacific WAVES – packages of POWER

ACTIVE ARCHITECT OF THE COASTLINE
Given birth a thousand miles or more at sea, waves slide through the water as on a frictionless conveyor. Expending their massive energies against the headlands and beaches, they cut away promontories and move tons of sand back and forth.

The broad, unobstructed expanse of the Pacific Ocean
spawns waves far more powerful than their Atlantic
counterparts. Unceasingly they break in a rhythmic beat
of surf that begins where the sea floor shallows. The
way waves approach the land tells much about the
offshore topography. Several lines of breakers indicate
parallel sand bars; lower and higher areas of waves
point out troughs and ridges in the bottom; waves that
rise and collapse suddenly signal a steep slope.

The placid waves of summer gradually pick up sand
from submerged bars to extend the beachfront, only to
have it stripped away and returned to the bars by the
violent waves of a winter storm. Responding to far off
cataclysms, the ocean can rear up in tidal waves. But
waves can also touch the shore with a gentle hand,
sculpting fingerlike cusps in the sand and leaving the
beach patterned with delicate ripples and rills.

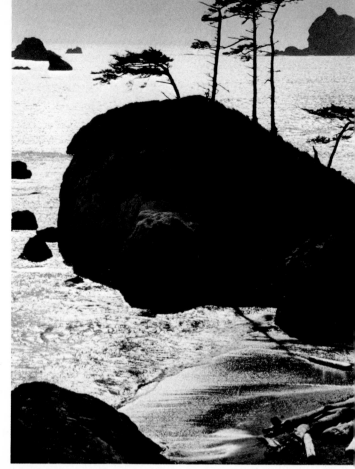

**CUTTING AND WEATHERING—
AGENTS OF EROSION**
*Sea stacks, right, are created when erosion
and wave action join forces to wear away
softer portions of a terraced coast, leaving
arches (see page 131) whose tops eventually
collapse. Like a horizontal saw, waves cut
into the land, chewing holes in cliff faces,
creating caves and tunnels, below, and
polishing rough rocks into smooth cobbles.*

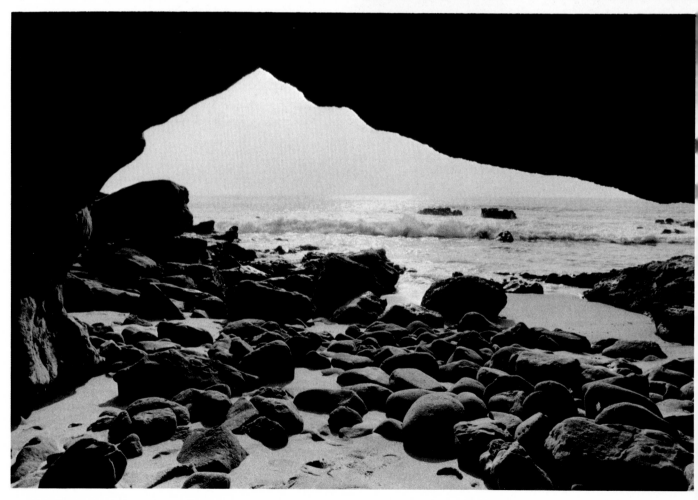

Where a beach has a gradual upward slope—as on most Southern California strands—waves roll in, retaining a smooth, rounded crest until their inshore end overbalances and spills down the advancing face, producing a curling front.

THE STUFF THAT SURFERS SEEK *Rocky shores (pages 240-241) cause waves to break apart in violent explosions of water and air.*

WHAT MAKES WAVES?

Most waves are caused by wind pushing the surface of the open sea into wrinkles. The water moves up and down with passage of a parcel of energy whose path forms a circular orbit (shown by curved arrows). In the shoaling zone, bottom friction slows a wave until its height and steepness increase to the extent that it breaks forward, creating surf. Undertow is the seaward return of water under the backwash.

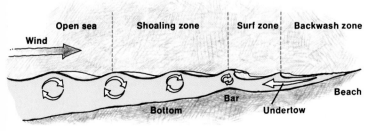

Open sea   Shoaling zone   Surf zone   Backwash zone

Wind

Bottom   Bar   Undertow   Beach

BULWARKS
and breakwaters
defend the
battered SHORE

GOOD BASIS
FOR PROTECTION
No, they aren't foundations for houses that haven't been built, nor are they underpinnings for a great pyramid. The concrete structures that separate land from water are the equivalent of a rocky cliff, and they are designed to protect softer material from erosion by absorbing the shock of pounding waves. Without protective seawalls, the bluff would gradually wear out from under the homes.

Endlessly the sea chews at the shoreline, wearing away at new land that is thrust up by an active earth and transporting it to new sites. The process is a natural one, but as man intensively develops the coastline, the shifting shore becomes a threat to himself and his investments. In attempts to forestall the processes of nature, up go a variety of defenses, usually formed from rock and concrete. Groins, which run across the beach into the water, are meant to trap sand and stabilize the beach. Jetties extend seaward from the mouths of rivers and harbors to prevent shoaling. Breakwaters create calm anchorages and protect the shore from wave action.

But such defenses often create greater problems than those they are intended to alleviate. The low walls of groins, jetties, and breakwaters obstruct the currents that carry sand along the shore. The slowed water drops its load, starving beaches farther down the coast and causing them to erode quickly. Some sand will eventually spill around groins to continue its journey, but much must be dredged and pumped around jetties and breakwaters to keep intact beaches to the south.

For those with the ocean in their front yard, seawalls slow cliff erosion, dikes keep water out of land reclaimed from the sea, broken rock and tetrapods soften the pounding of the surf.

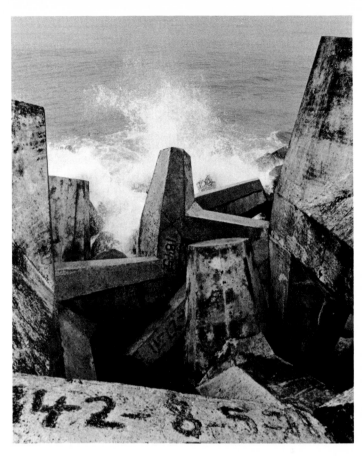

JUMBLE OF JACKSTONES
Energy of waves slamming into a jumble of huge tetrapods, above, is dissipated in turbulence. Such concrete monsters—each weighing more than forty tons—are cast on site and placed in interlocking layers over a core of natural stone and concrete. Left: Broken stones loosely thrown together— called riprap—disperse force of pounding surf, even though very heavy waves can toss them around like pebbles.

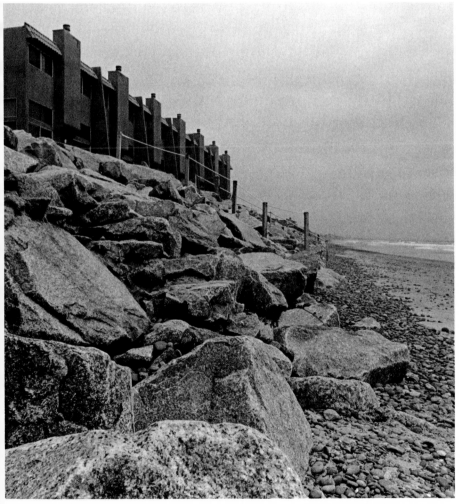

BOATING
is the name of
the GAME

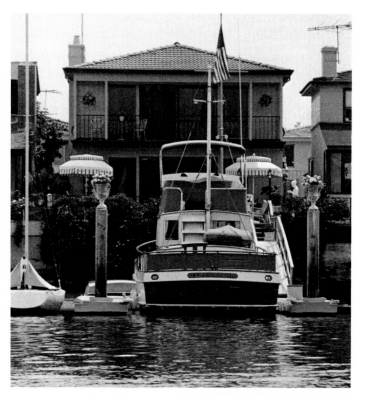

From Long Beach to Laguna Beach, pleasure boating is big business. More than a dozen major fiberglass boat builders and numerous smaller ones cluster in the area, making it the small boat capital of the nation. They sell to a populace that eagerly takes to the water in craft ranging from skitterish racing dinghies to monumental motor cruisers, seeking yet another recreational escape and perhaps some measure of intermittent solitude on the rolling sea.

Each weekend the multitude weighs anchor for coastal waterways, and solitude becomes but a word. Luxury power yachts, more like second homes than boats, cast off from private docks for a harbor sortie or a trip to one of the channel islands (Catalina is an all-time favorite). Eight-foot Naples Sabots, the most numerous class in the region, bob like peanut shells around buoys in sheltered water, skippered by junior sailors and old salts whose knees sometimes stick up high above the gunnels. Offshore yachts hoist colorful spinnakers during regattas. Most local races center on Catalina; a few favorites end in Mexico. And every other Fourth of July, sleek ocean racers from several countries leave Long Beach for a quick ride on the trade winds to Hawaii.

HOME ON THE HARBOR
In the watery world of Newport Bay, a cabin cruiser nestles contentedly in its landscaped slip, above. Out in Lido Channel, right, sailing conditions are crowded, and a catamaran squeezes by a sloop.

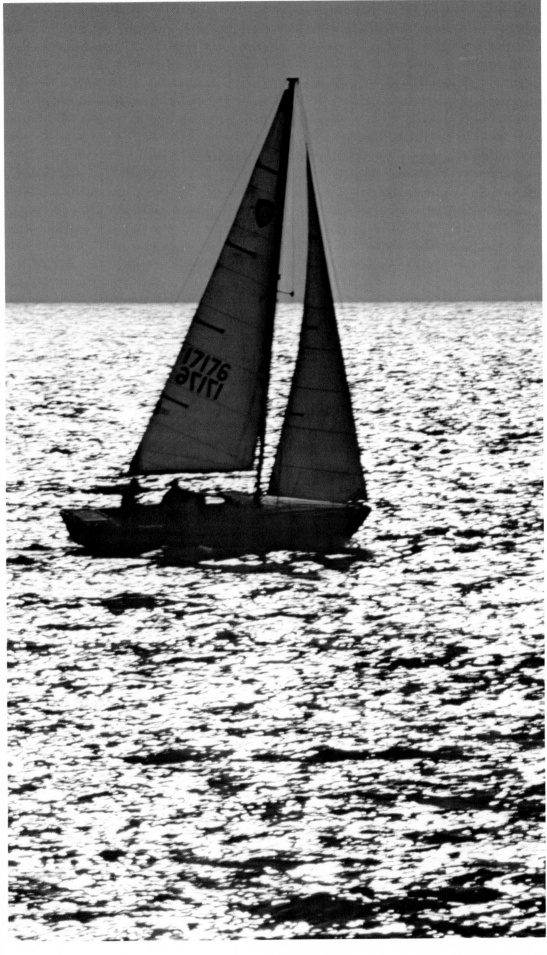

A BEAUTIFUL
PEA-GREEN BOAT
Working to weather on a
reflective sea off Redondo
Beach, a close-hauled sloop
glides under smoggy skies
the color of split-pea soup.

WHERE HAVE ALL THE SKIPPERS GONE? *Looking like a school of guppies, hundreds of cruisers and sailboats sit idly at their moorings in Dana Point Marina. With its artificial breakwaters and manmade island, the harbor is a far cry from the way it must have looked when seaman Henry Dana viewed it from the brig Pilgrim (facing page).*

"Down this height we pitched the hides..."

Working up and down the California coast in the hide and tallow trade, Richard Henry Dana (pp. 141, 281) found himself in many ports. San Juan (later to be known as Dana Point)—made a strong impression on his mind.

"Coasting along on the quiet shore of the Pacific, we came to anchor in twenty fathoms' water, almost out at sea, as it were, and directly abreast of a steep hill which overhung the water, and was twice as high as our royal-mast-head. We had heard much of this place from the Lagoda's crew, who said it was the worst place in California. The shore is rocky, and directly exposed to the south-east, so that vessels are obliged to slip and run for their lives on the first sign of a gale. . . .

"San Juan's is the only romantic spot in California. The country here for several miles is high table-land, running boldly to the shore, and breaking off in a steep hill, at the foot of which the waters of the Pacific are constantly dashing. For several miles the water washes the very base of the hill, or breaks upon ledges and fragments of rocks which run out into the sea. Just where we landed was a small cove, or 'bight,' which gave us, at high tide, a few square feet of sand-beach between the sea and the bottom of the hill. . . . Directly before us, rose the perpendicular height of four or five hundred feet. How we were to get hides down, or goods up, upon the table-land on which the mission was situated, was more than we could tell. The agent had taken a long circuit, and yet had frequently to jump over breaks, and climb up steep places, in the ascent. No animal but a man or a monkey could get up it. . . .

"There was a grandeur in everything around, which gave almost a solemnity to the scene: a silence and solitariness which affected everything! Not a human being but ourselves for miles; and no sound heard but the pulsations of the great Pacific! and the great steep hill rising like a wall, and cutting us off from all the world. . . . Compared with the plain, dull sand-beach of the rest of the coast, this grandeur was as refreshing as a great rock in a weary land. . . .

". . . we came to the top. Here the country stretched out for miles, as far as the eye could reach, on a level, table surface; and the only habitation in sight was the small white mission of San Juan Capistrano, with a few Indian huts about it, standing in a small hollow about a mile from where we were. . . .

"Down this height we pitched the hides, throwing them as far out into the air as we could; and as they were all large, stiff, and doubled, like the cover of a book, the wind took them, and they swayed and eddied about, plunging and rising in the air, like a kite when it has broken its string. As it was now low tide, there was no danger of their falling into the water, and as fast as they came to ground, the men below picked them up, and taking them on their heads, walked off with them to the boat. It was really a picturesque sight: the great height; the scaling of the hides; and the continual walking to and fro of the men who looked like mites, on the beach!"

For the SAFETY of the southern MARINER

During Spanish Colonial days, officials in San Diego hung a lantern from a stake at Ballast Point whenever a supply ship was due. But it wasn't until the mid-1800s that Southern California had its first lighthouses: welcoming lights at Point Loma in San Diego and Santa Barbara and a warning light at treacherous Point Conception. None of these three original lights is still in use. The Point Loma beacon, which was too often obscured by clouds on its lofty vantage point, was replaced by a skeleton tower at a lower level. In 1882 another lighthouse in Point Conception rose in place of the first, which had settled and cracked. In 1925 an earthquake finally toppled the Santa Barbara tower.

NOT PICTURESQUE . . .
BUT FUNCTIONAL
Constructed in 1913 and containing a lens that today is almost a hundred years old, Los Angeles light stands stolidly at the end of the long breakwater that protects Los Angeles Harbor. Automated light, fog signal, and radio beacon all are monitored from Long Beach.

CABLE CROSSING

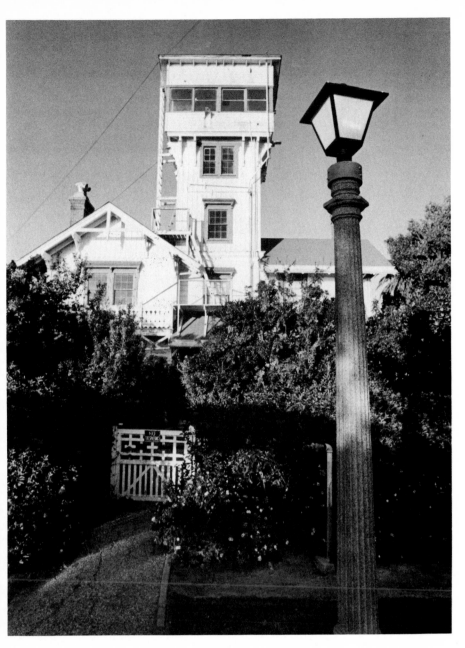

NOT FUNCTIONAL . . . BUT PICTURESQUE

Pioneer lighthouse at Point Fermin—built in 1874—looks across Los Angeles Harbor to distant mountains and across the sea to Catalina. Constructed of lumber and brick brought around the Horn, the Victorian building is now an historic monument, its lighthouse duty taken over by a beacon located at edge of nearby cliff.

LIGHTS IN THE NIGHT

Spotted from Point Arguello to San Diego, Southern California light stations are administered by Eleventh Coast Guard District, based at Long Beach. Many stations have radio beacons, in addition to a light and foghorn. Mariners who can't hear or see a station can take bearings of two radio beacons and discover where they are by locating point where lines intersect.

*THE OLD LIGHTHOUSE
AT POINT LOMA*
*No longer active, the
spic-and-span lighthouse
atop Point Loma is a
museum of the life and
times of one of its keepers
—Captain Robert Israel—
who lived there with his
family. In the kitchen a table
is set for dinner, complete
with jam pot and toothpicks.
In children's room, toys
are scattered about as
if dropped but
a moment before.*

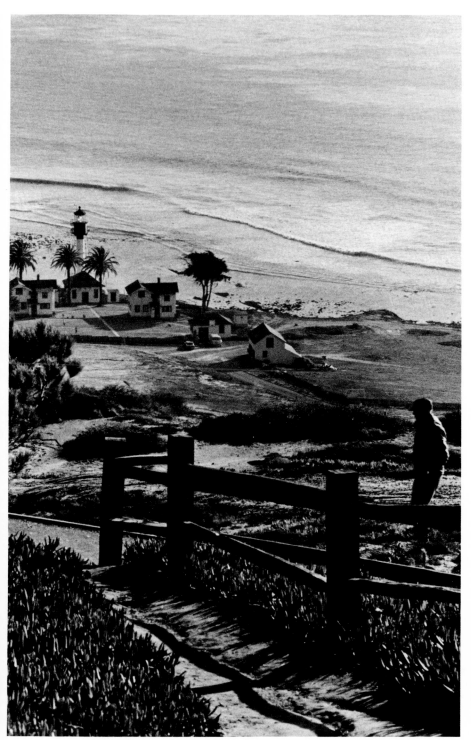

THE "NEW" SAN DIEGO LIGHT

Because low clouds frequently obscured original beacon that was on higher ground, San Diego's light was moved to its present site at water's edge in 1891. Even when fog is thick, horizontal rays from a light —created by panels in the lens (see page 129)—can be seen by ships as flashes.

BLAIR STAPP

DETOUR
to departed glory—
the CAPISTRANO MISSION

SIDETRIP TO OLD SPAIN
Only three miles from the Coast Highway, the village of San Juan Capistrano preserves colorful touches of its Spanish and Mexican heritage. Few are as harmonious or mellow as its venerable mission, founded in 1776 by Father Junipero Serra. Even on warm, visitor-busy days, the arcade surrounding the patio is quiet and cool.

A continent away from the battlefields of the American Revolution, the declining empire of Spain, in its belated attempt to colonize the territory of Alta California, established the seventh in a chain of 21 missions—San Juan Capistrano. Through the years that the young nation to the east was pushing across the Great Plains, the missions also flourished. But in 1833 the government in Mexico ordered them secularized, and the resulting turmoil destroyed both Capistrano's prosperity and its very walls.

A few structures in the present surrounding town have tried to emulate the simple grace of the mission, which once was a complete city in itself, embracing nearly two acres of land. Preservation efforts at the mission have restored a serene elegance and a strong feeling of the past for anyone who will pause along the colonnades to contemplate the weathered, ivy-covered walls.

AS RENOWNED AS THE SWALLOWS *Campanario is at end of a tranquil garden adjoining "Father Serra's church," the only remaining place where the founder of California's missions is known to have said Mass. A sign asks visitors not to ring ancient bells, which have become as widely celebrated as Capistrano's swallows.*

San Diego's

The Sunny Coast—"...a little

A word often used to sum up the character of the San Diego shore is "diversified." Yet words are elusive representations, especially since this region diffuses a charm more readily experienced than described.

A sparkling climate blesses the San Diego shore, helping to create an unusual combination of recreation and natural resource. But climate is only part of the story. From the busy beaches at the county's upper end to the undeveloped Tijuana estuary, California's southern shore is a pleasureable place for resident and visitor alike.

At the top of this coastal segment, Camp Pendleton forms a buffer against potential encroachment by urbanization reaching out from Orange County. Though most of the military base is inaccessible to the public, its tenants—the Marine Corps—point with justifiable pride to their having instituted a nationally acclaimed program of wildlife habitat preservation.

Regional pride is expressed by most residents of the upper coastal communities. Even those from other parts of California exhibit a mutual concern for the area's valuable natural resources.

In a travel-oriented society, La Jolla is an oasis of another sort, working hard at *not* attracting visitors. Farther south, tourism is the reason for the remarkable Mission Bay Complex. And such commercial diversions as offered by San Diego Bay fade to insignificance in the sparse but natural coastal landscape near the Mexican border.

Shore

"more grace, a little more charm"

I have been to San Diego, a nice
little spot in the corner of the
United States where the climate
is delightful and Oranges, Lemons,
Figs, Olives, and all Semi-tropical
productions flourish. . . .

—George Phillips Marston

SUNNING KNOWS
NO SEASON

On a sparkling day—and there are plenty of them for most of the year—sun worshippers sprout like weeds along the beaches. The sea is why people come to the north county coast, and the sea is why people keep coming back. Reveling in retirement in Leucadia, a native Arizonian declared: "People come over here from Riverside, San Bernardino, Los Angeles. It's the best beach area anywhere."

COMBING the county's north COAST

Unbroken miles of sand string together a series of sun-drenched coastside towns that dot the shore from the Orange County line almost to San Diego. Oceanside, Carlsbad, Leucadia, Encinitas, Cardiff by the Sea, Solana Beach, Del Mar—they are quiet communities, founded principally as resorts and now popular with retirees. An outsider cannot see a whit of difference between one township strand and another; his unjaundiced eye makes them all out to be equally captivating. But with wry regional pride, residents of each area claim superiority for their beach over those immediately to the north or south.

"Ours is better kept and less crowded," they say.

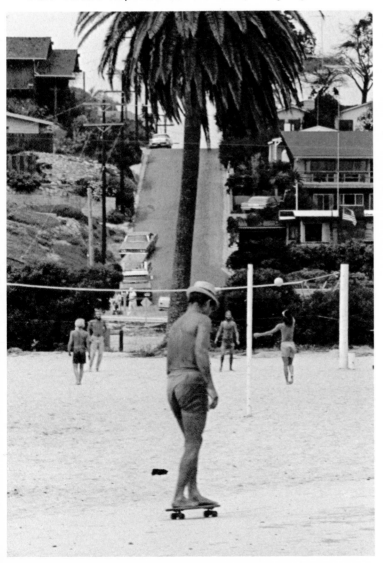

ENOUGH SUN FOR EVERYONE
Enjoying a whiz of a ride, a skate board enthusiast ends a long traverse down a street that is matter-of-factly interrupted by palm trees and a volley ball net at Encinitas' Moonlight Beach, left. Farther along the same shore, grotesquely eroded sandstone bluffs fascinate but hardly deter a determined stroller, above.

SHORE OF THE SUNDOWN SEA... That's what writer T. H. Watkins calls California's coast. Morning sun peeking over the Santa Margarita Mountains transforms the sea at San Onofre to dancing liquid silver. But the shore's evening mood is more meditative. Then, a golden haze suffuses both land and sea, spreading a radiance that glows long after the sun slips below the horizon.

DICK ROWAN

...WHERE THE TURF MEETS THE SURF
The San Diego shore is salubrious for both man and beast. Every morning during eight weeks of summer, sleek thoroughbreds run the beaches and romp in the surf prior to thrilling thousands of fans at famed Del Mar track, opposite.

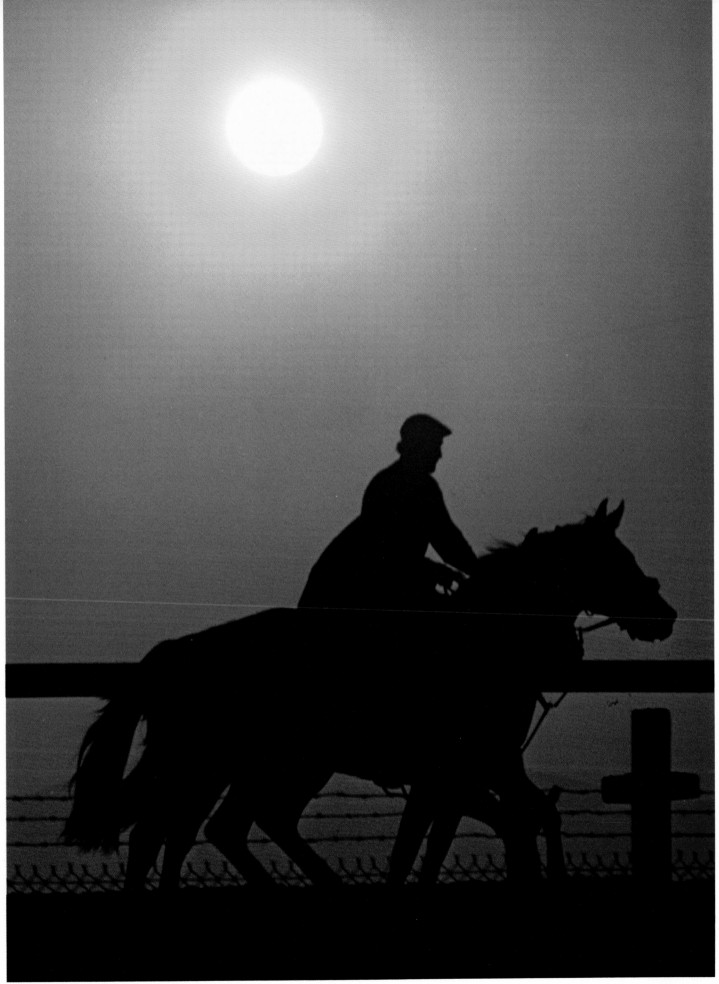

THOMAS MAHNKEN

FISSION
by the sea-the task
of taming the ATOM

DIABLO CANYON'S BIG DOME
Seven miles south of San Luis Obispo, Diablo Canyon nuclear power center offers a back-country bus tour to an overlook of plant site near water's edge, left. Diablo's visitor center features many fascinating exhibits that help clarify the concept of nuclear power. Right: Cranking keeps a panel of lights bright, but you'd have to keep at it for 13 hours to generate a penny's worth of electricity.

Nuclear power is nothing new along California's western edge. At Humboldt Bay, fission was put to work making electricity in 1963. Four years later the coast's second nuclear power station began production at San Onofre. A third facility at Diablo Canyon is slated to go into operation in 1976-77.

Since these nuclear generators are cooled by an elaborate system that gulps in and spits out huge quantities of water, they are erected near the ocean. But the extreme pressure of water moving through a plant—and its temperature increase—can destroy indigenous marine life. Contention also festers about atomic energy's potential radiation hazards.

GERALD FREDRICK

SAN ONOFRE'S
POWER AND GLORY
*Tennis ball dome that
houses reactor of San
Onofre generating station is
familiar sight to motorists
heading along State 5 south
of San Clemente. San
Onofre's first nuclear unit
has a net generating
capacity of 430 megawatts;
two additional units—under
construction in 1974—will
increase capacity fivefold,
producing enough
electricity to supply a city of
over two million people.*

HOW NUCLEAR POWER WORKS
*Fission (splitting) of atoms in nuclear fuel creates heat, which
boils water, producing high-pressure steam. Jetting into
turbine, steam strikes fanlike blades, spinning generator rotor
—a giant electromagnet. The mechanical motion creates
electric current, which travels along power lines to
consumers. Sea water is used to cool steam back to distilled
water. Control rods start or stop fissioning.*

Torrey Pines: A Primitive Pocket of Unique Beauty

Protected from commercial developments and adapted to major geologic changes, a rare tree now fights only wind and drought.

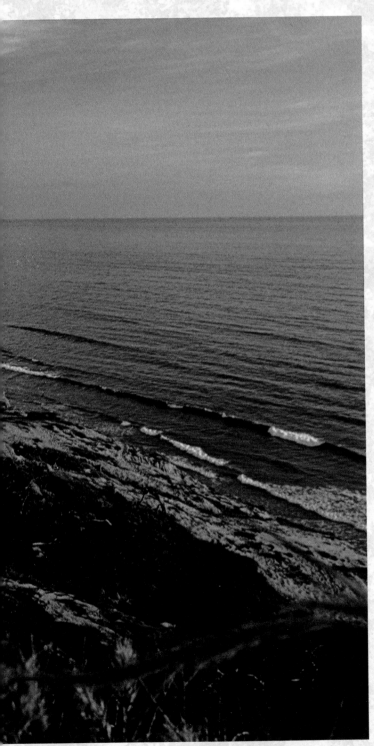

The roots of the Torrey pine reach as deeply into the soil as they do into time. Clinging tenaciously to parched bluffs, the last stands of this rarest of pines grow on Santa Rosa Island and in a state reserve on the coast north of La Jolla.

In 1850 the fragile status of the trees was recognized by conservation-minded citizens. Efforts to preserve the Torrey pines were intense but followed a haphazard course until the final additions to the reserve were authorized in 1970. In the years between, the city council of San Diego leased the lands for grazing. Pines were cleared and burned for fuel, and fires swept the denuded areas. Tracts were sold to private owners, who began to draw up plans for development. This was stymied by the purchase of several hundred acres by the wealthy benefactress, Ellen B. Scripps, but a new danger had to be contended with: campers and picnickers chopping the trees for firewood. Housing subdivisions now abut the reserve boundaries where the race between developers and the Torrey pine's supporters ended. Although man cannot guarantee the trees' survival, he has at least left them an arena where they continue to battle against extinction.

A MONUMENT FASHIONED BY NATURE
Sunset gloriously illuminates the deeply eroded, 300-foot cliffs of Torrey Pines. Almost over the horizon, La Jolla gleams like a collection of polished pebbles. Sage, buckwheat, spice bush, and other native shrubs thrive among the pines and in the canyons; springtime sees the mesa brilliantly carpeted with wildflowers right out to the cliff edge.

FAT MAN'S
MISERY
Negotiable only by beanpole bodies, a tortuous path beginning at Red Butte worms its way between sandstone bluffs, in some places hardly more than a foot apart. Once you're into the passage, it's best to move right along without thinking of such things as falling rocks or earthquakes. Portions of the trail thread past exposed roots and twisted branches of the venerable Torrey Pine.

CLIFF SAILER'S DELIGHT

Just beyond the southern terminus of Torrey Pines Reserve is a coastal stretch that is put to a number of good uses. At foot of cliffs—where the binoculars are pointed—is Black's Beach, a place of natural, nude exuberance. Centipede pier in middle distance belongs to Scripps Institution of Oceanography, marine laboratory for the University of California. Upsweeping sea breezes, deflected by the cliffs, create a midair mecca for sailplane and hang glider zealots. The varied ways of gliders are illustrated below.

Vertical air currents

Strong winds

High mountains

Hot valleys

Coastal cliffs

Sea breezes

Thermal Riding. Vertical air currents, or updrafts, caused by uneven heating of ground by sun, permit long cross-country flights. Thermal riding is done mostly in inland valleys during the summer months.

Wave Soaring. Strong winds over mountain ranges form rolling turbulence in lee of high mountains. Some wave soaring is done along back of coastal range, but most is on east side of Sierra Nevada.

Cliff Sailing. Sea breezes flow up and over high coastside cliffs, making cushion of air currents for sailplanes, hang gliders (small object near cliff edge).

Pleasures and PAINS of coastside LIVING

What are some of the amenities that make people willing to pay the price of waterfront real estate? An unobstructed view of the sea's infinite faces; a feeling of living in close touch with nature; a breath of fresh air; a gentle climate given only occasionally to fits of temper; a handy playground. For all of these reasons and many more, the pleasure of having the ocean as a neighbor is a highly coveted one.

Unfortunately, a dream house by the sea can cause a few nightmares, too. Salt borne by spray coats windows and corrodes paint. Beach dwellers may wake up to find only an expanse of cobbles, the sand having been temporarily stripped by a storm. And the weather doesn't always live up to expectations. In spite of California's sunny reputation, there are bleak winter weeks of overcast or fog.

Perhaps the most serious problem of seaside living is erosion. Homes may be built on beaches that are naturally receding or that are being starved by such obstructions as dams and breakwaters. Clifftop homes may accelerate the already active processes that wear away their foundations. The simple factor of added weight may cause unstable bluffs to shift and crumble. Lawn sprinkling adds excess ground water that percolates through the cliff and increases the risk of slumping. In some instances, water running off roofs has channeled in such a way as to carve ditches in the cliff face.

The answers to erosion for existing homes are sand hauls to replenish beaches, and seawalls or piles of broken rock at cliff bases. In the future, the ultimate solution may be to declare a buffer zone between civilization and sea.

WILL IT OR WON'T IT?
Celebrated for their sweeping seascapes— as well as their unstable bluffs—Santa Monica and neighboring Pacific Palisades sometimes pay for their proximity to the ocean. Supersaturated ground material— created by irrigation— and torrential rains cause large chunks of earth to drop away, not infrequently carrying sizeable portions of once horizontal real estate down to the Coast Highway.

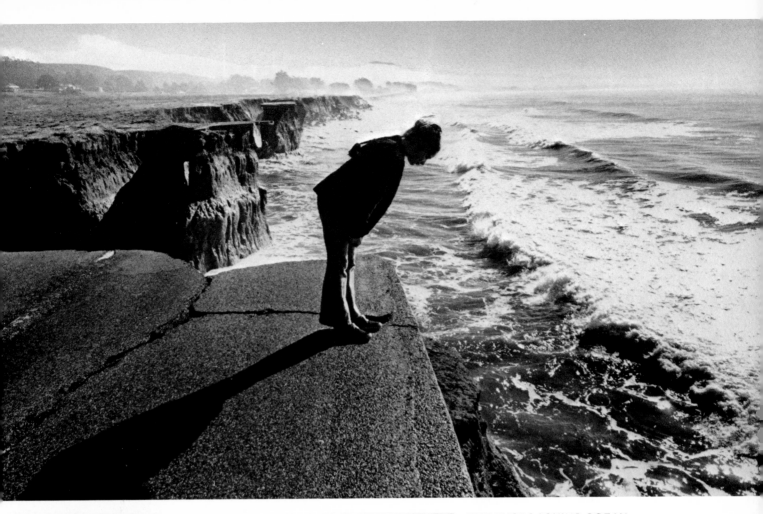

THE ENCROACHING OCEAN
Paved highway once ran all along the Princeton shore, just south of San Francisco. The surging sea has taken great bites of the land, above, causing portions of two-lane to collapse and isolating slabs of asphalt atop crumbling stacks of soil. Left: Cliffs near Del Mar (San Diego County) are furrowed by water runoff and wave action. Without some kind of control, land slumping and sloughing off of bluff material will continue.

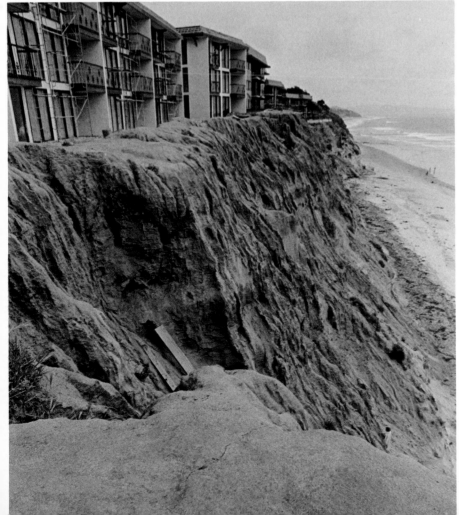

Two-week summer vacations began with the new century, offering a respite from hot cities and often harsh working conditions. Americans flocked to the seashore to frolic in the sea air and salt water. Back then, however, beach fashions were more restrained—and more restraining. A good many sand strollers wore everyday garments, the ladies only sometimes daring to lift their skirts and wet their toes. The more venturesome arrived in cumbersome costumes that must have kept their wearers close to shore for fear of drowning. By the 1920s women had begun leaving less to modesty and more to sunburn, appearing in the clinging, knee-length swim suits previously worn only by men.

SUNNY PLACES . . .
HAPPY FACES
Sporting turn-of-the-century high fashion, ladies and gentlemen take the sea air at San Diego's Coronado Beach in 1903. Middy blouse outfits of stiff linen or scratchy wool preserved a modicum of modesty and prevented an overdose of sun. In lower photo, a gallant soldier—who would have nothing to do with the water—stands by lady friends with one umbrella while his barracks' mate reposes under another.

By the
SEA,
by the beautiful
SEA

THE GOOD OLD SUMMERTIME
Dressed in 1914-style Sunday best, a family heads for shoot-the-chute thrills at San Diego's Wonderland Park, though big sister seems to have some misgivings about the whole idea. Below: Looking as if just let out of church, a smartly clad crowd strolls and sits the sands of Ocean Beach, wistfully gazing seaward at the more daring surf bathers.

TITLE INSURANCE AND TRUST CO.

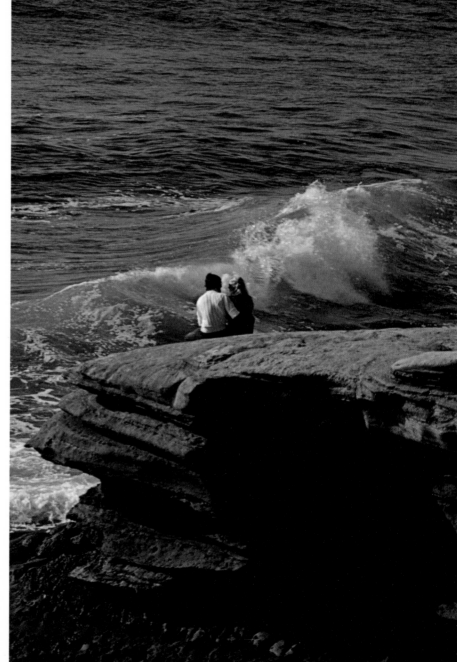

LOOK . . . BUT DON'T TOUCH

Momentarily oblivious to natural beauties, a couple shares an intimate moment at the surging sea near Goldfish Point, southern boundary of San Diego-La Jolla Underwater Park. The ecological reserve was established to preserve the shoreline and underwater life of La Jolla Canyon. Sea life may be observed—but not disturbed.

LA JOLLA is not the usual TOURIST place

The casual but refined feeling pervading La Jolla is wholly suited to the town's dual personality: it is strong in both recreation and research.

From its early days as a beach resort, La Jolla's atmosphere has been consciously maintained. Old shingled cottages still stand along the shaded streets, and most of the other buildings keep a low architectural profile. Good shops and restaurants abound. But the town has resisted such appeals to mass tourism as amusement parks, rows of hotels, and glittering night life.

Instead, La Jolla has gained world fame as a center for research. Scripps Institution of Oceanography is a leader in the field of marine study. A little north of Scripps rises the Salk Institute for Biological Studies, an interdisciplinary think tank named for the pioneer in polio vaccine.

Anyone coming for beach fun will find that La Jolla can match the best. From the quiet waters and intimate strand of La Jolla Cove to the celebrated surf of Windansea, the shore still beguiles with the same charm that induced early-century vacationers to linger here.

THE COVE—STEADFAST SEASIDE SYMBOL
Sea beauty is the reason for everything else at La Jolla. Since 1866 visitors have been coming all the way from the east coast to enjoy the ocean and the shore. Condominium with an ocean outlook fronts on "the cove," area's most popular swimming and sunbathing spot.

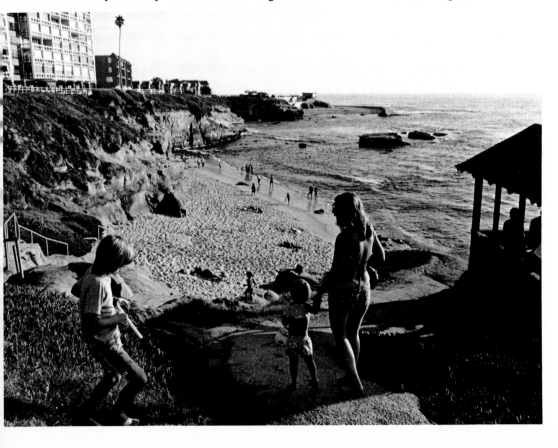

A LIFEGUARD'S
day is not
always SUNNY

The lifeguards of the southland dispel the old stereotype of a sun-bronzed Apollo surrounded by a covey of admiring females. To be sure, lifeguards are conspicuously present (and often bronzed and handsome), but to the benefit of the multitudes that throng the shore, they are also active, efficient, and dedicated. Many guards are full-time professionals; all receive rigorous training in rescue and advanced first aid and even a few tips on maintaining good public relations. Much of a lifeguard's day involves routine patrolling, locating strayed children, and treating assorted wounds and cuts. Lifeguards also perform cliff rescues, deliver babies, and give talks on beach safety and marine life to scout groups and schools. Summer Sundays keep them busiest, for then they most often dash into the surf to aid swimmers in distress.

SIGN OF TIMES— AND TIDES
Updated frequently, a chalkboard at main lifeguard tower informs beach users of water conditions. To keep information current, guards periodically cruise the shore in jeeps containing rescue equipment and first-aid supplies. At some beaches, guards are authorized to issue citations to refractory visitors, though a spirit of public cooperation usually prevails.

WAVE WATCHING—WITH A PURPOSE *"Gentlemen, please move your surfboards to the south. You are now in a swimming area." In addition to safety, rescue, and policing duties, guards provide first-aid for cuts, bruises, jellyfish stings, stingray wounds. Main tower is linked by radio to Coast Guard, police, hospital, ambulance service. During summer season at heavily used beaches, some stations are manned 24 hours.*

SAN DIEGO'S
enduring bond with the SEA

Less intense, more genteel, and more attuned to the tides than to the rush of progress, California's oldest city keeps a pace of its own. Surrounding the long, hooked bay that gave it birth, San Diego acknowledges that its lifeblood is still the sea. The Pacific Fleet makes its home in the exceptional harbor, and naval ships and installations are omnipresent. Enough ocean freighters call at commercial docks to make the city a respectable port, and close to a hundred oceanographic organizations find the location particularly suited to their research.

San Diego differs from many ports in that this city's waterfront is an inviting center. The Embarcadero is tidy, the water is clean, and the harbor has been planned for recreation as well as for business. The largest fishing fleet in the United States leaves from San Diego to seine for tuna as far south as Chile. Many Navy officers find the bay so to their liking that they retire in the town of Coronado on North Island.

Just north of the harbor is Mission Bay, a 4,600-acre aquatic playground where water activities are carefully orchestrated to fit simultaneously into a maze of manmade channels.

But to many visitors the city's best is still the grand old Hotel del Coronado. Thomas Edison himself supervised installation of the hotel's electric lighting in 1894. And since 1888 the rambling Victorian structure has hosted distinguished dignitaries from around the world. They come to enjoy the heritage of San Diego—the sea.

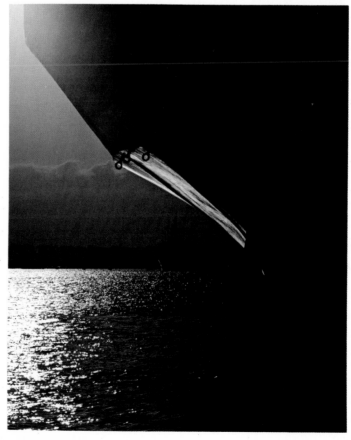

CENTURY-OLD SEADOG
Catching the sun with her figurehead and a Navy vessel with her stern, Star of India—oldest merchantman afloat—is preserved as a historical relic on the waterfront.

SEA . . . PLUS SHADES OF SPAIN
Facing page: Tile roofs and tower of St. Joseph Cathedral are a reminder of Spanish days of discovery, when—in 1769— the first link in chain of California missions was forged near San Diego Bay. Presence of numerous companies and institutions engaged in ocean research has given San Diego the name of oceanographic capital of the world.

LAY OF THE BAY

Finger-shaped bay is closed at lower end by thin neck of Silver Strand. The Navy is everywhere, from submarine pens and fueling depots on Point Loma to the Air Station on Coronado's North Island and the mothball fleet moored in the south bay.

SEAPORT CITY

As seen from Harbor Island, skyscrapers punctuate the city skyline at east edge of bay. Both Harbor Island and Shelter Island (see map) were built from material dredged from harbor bottom. Despite its heavy use, San Diego Bay is one of world's cleanest.

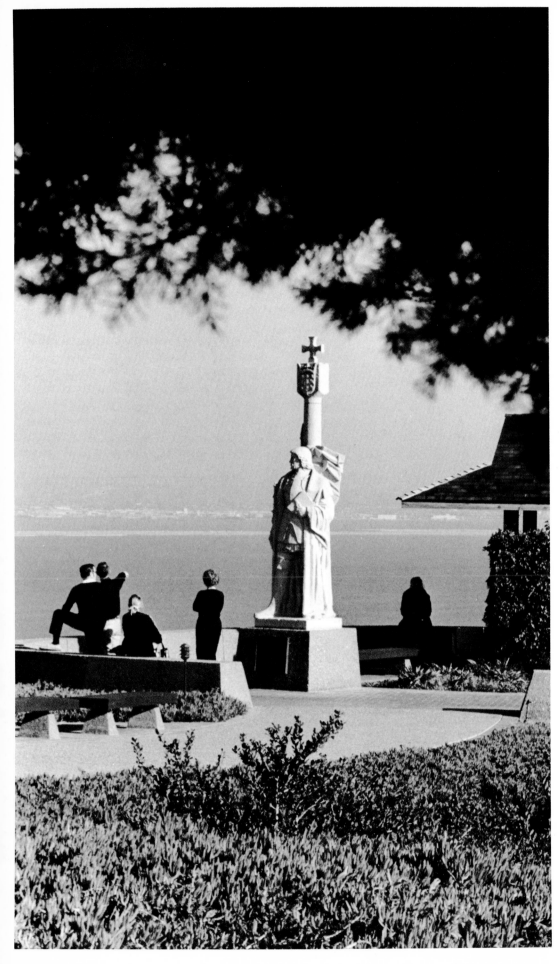

"A VERY GOOD AND ENCLOSED PORT"
Arriving on the day of St. Michael the Archangel, in 1542, Portuguese seafarer Juan Cabrillo named the bay San Miguel. Not until early 1600s was the discoverer's "good port" renamed—by Basque explorer Sebastian Viscaino, who went ashore on what he thought was the feast day of St. Diego (he actually landed the day before). Discovery of California coast is credited to Cabrillo, whose statue stands at Point Loma.

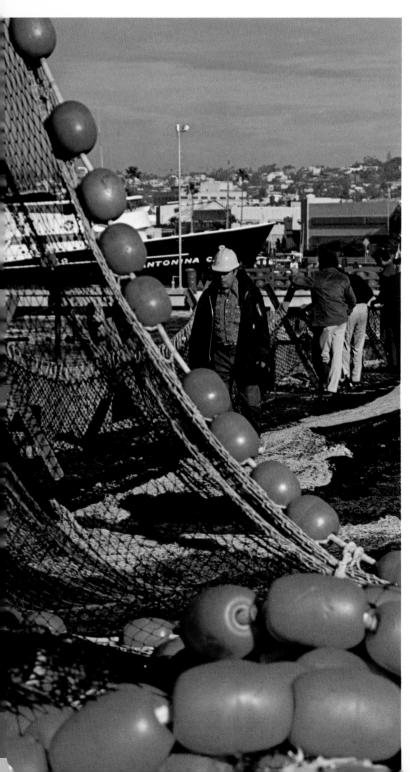

TWO WAYS
ON TWO BAYS

Cat-rigged sailboats await rental use in a stiff breeze at Mission Bay, above, an aquatic wonderland featuring playgrounds, beaches, golf courses, and Sea World, an enthralling oceanarium. Concentration—not recreation —is order of the day when San Diego's far-ranging tuna fleet is in port, left. Net mending goes on at foot of Broadway.

"The Indians came down early, with horses..."

In the mid-1800s, California's principal harbors were San Francisco, Monterey, San Pedro, San Diego. Richard Henry Dana (see pp. 141, 249) was not impressed with San Diego but admitted to its practical qualities.

"We sailed leisurely down the coast before a light, fair wind, keeping the land well aboard, and saw two other missions, looking like blocks of white plaster, shining in the distance; one of which, situated on the top of a high hill was San Louis Rey, which the third mate said was only fifteen miles from San Diego. At sunset on the second day, we had a large and well wooded headland directly before us, behind which lay the little harbor of San Diego. We were becalmed off this point all night, but the next morning . . . having a good breeze, we stood round the point, and hauling our wind, brought the little harbor, which is rather the outlet of a small river, right before us. Every one was anxious to get a view of the new place. A chain of high hills, beginning at the point. . . . protected the harbor on the north and west, and ran off into the interior, as far as the eye could reach. On the other sides, the land was low, and green, but without trees. The entrance is so narrow as to admit but one vessel at a time, the current swift, and the channel runs so near to a low stony point that the ship's sides appeared almost to touch it. There was no town in sight, but on the smooth sand beach, abreast, and within a cable's length of which three vessels lay moored, were four large houses . . . with piles of hides standing 'round them, and men in red shirts and large straw hats, walking in and out of the doors. These were the hide houses. . . .

"Our crew fell in with some who belonged to the other vessels, and sailor-like, steered for the first grog-shop. This was a small mud building, of only one room, in which were liquors, dry and West India goods, shoes, bread, fruits, and everything which is vendible in California. It was kept by a Yankee, a one-eyed man, who . . . came out to the Pacific in a whale-ship, left her at the Sandwich Islands, and came to California. . . .

"The small settlement lay directly below the fort, composed of about forty dark brown looking huts, or houses, and two larger ones, plastered. . . . This town is not more than half as large as Monterey, or Santa Barbara, and has little or no business. . . .

"For landing and taking on board hides, San Diego is decidedly the best place in California. The harbor is small and land-locked; there is no surf; the vessels lie within a cable's length of the beach; and the beach itself is smooth, hard sand, without rocks or stones. For these reasons, it is used by all the vessels in the trade, as a depot. . . .

"This was the first Sunday that the crew had been in San Diego, and of course they were all for going up to see the town. The Indians came down early, with horses to let for the day, and all the crew, who could obtain liberty, went off to the presidio and mission, and did not return until night."

Coast WATCHING on a WHALE'S scale

The Moby Dick parade, as Californians call the gray whale's southern migration, has shattered the aura of awesome mystery given all whales by Herman Melville's white leviathan. Plucked back from the brink of extinction through international protection, the grays range between the Arctic Ocean and the Gulf of California, but their obliging habit of sticking close to the California shore has made them a familiar part of the coastal scene.

From the moment they heave in sight on their annual journey, gray whales have precious little privacy. During winter months, thousands of binocular-eyed spectators follow their passage from choice vantages or board chartered craft that cruise alongside the docile 30- to 45-tonners. Scientists trail the gray giants to their breeding grounds, subjecting them to more intense scrutiny than any other species of whale receives.

WATCHERS OF THE WHALE UNITE
Dispensing supportive enthusiasm in large measure, up-front whale watchers utilize binoculars, telescopes, camera lenses, and naked eyes to look for "spouts" of exhaled breath out at sea. During annual migration along the southern shore—from December through February—a favorite spotting site is the whale lookout station at the tip of Point Loma.

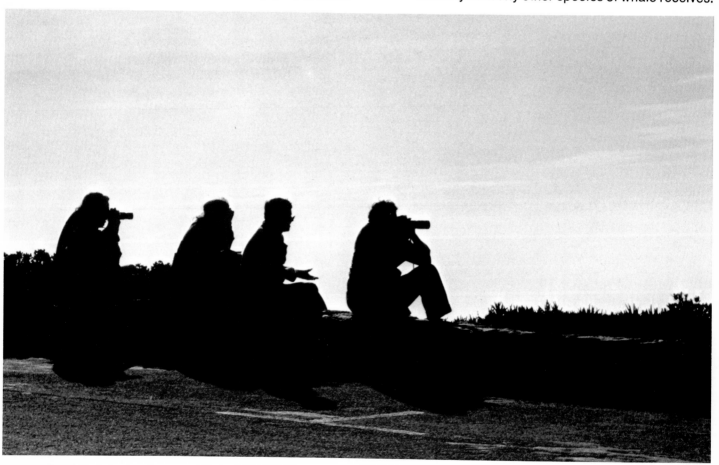

"THERE SHE GOES!"

Flukes fling skyward as a gray whale heads for the depths. Surfacing to breathe, a whale blasts a 10 to 15-foot "blow" of warm, humid air. After inhaling, it sinks gently like a submarine, or—more dramatically—throws flukes, thrusting its wide tail fins into the air before sounding to a hundred feet. Some conservationists claim that whale-watching boats harass the creatures, causing them to follow a coastal route farther out to sea each year.

THE WAY OF WHALES

From summer feeding grounds in the Bering Strait region of the Arctic, the California gray whale swims a 6,000-mile route south to breeding and calving lagoons on Mexico's west coasts. San Diego Bay was once a calving grounds, but the whaling industry ended that.

GULLS are greedy, gluttonous...and GRACEFUL

Screeching, they follow fishing boats in wheeling flocks; scrabbling, they alight on fishing piers to snatch up bait; squabbling, they descend in clouds on shoreside dumps. For a gull, it seems there is no further purpose to life beyond eating. But in spite of their catholic diet—or perhaps because of it—gulls have never been threatened by extinction. The 17 species that frequent the west coast thrive where man thrives, rudely feeding on his refuse. Their behavior notwithstanding, gulls are poetry in flight. Powerful and deliberate strokes of their long, wide wings propel them up to catch an air current. Then, soaring effortlessly, they are freed for the moment from the frenzied scrapping that characterizes a gull's more mundane affairs.

Selected Readings

The Natural World

Abbott, R. Tucker, *Seashells of North America.* Golden Press, 1968.

Abrams, Leroy, *Illustrated Flora of the Pacific States, 4 volumes.* Stanford, California, Stanford University Press, 1960.

Amos, William H., *The Life of the Seashore.* New York, Toronto, London, McGraw-Hill Book Company/The World Book Encyclopedia, 1966.

Bailey, Harry, *The Climate of Southern California.* Berkeley, University of California Press, 1966.

Bascom, Willard, *Waves & Beaches, The Dynamics of the Ocean Surface.* Garden City, New York, Anchor Books, Doubleday & Company, Inc., 1964.

Baxter, John L., *Inshore Fishes.* California Department of Fish & Game, 1966.

Berrill, N. J., *The Life of the Ocean.* New York, Toronto, London, McGraw-Hill Book Company, 1966.

——, *The Living Tide.* Fawcett, 1951.

Bonnot, Paul, *The Sea Lions, Seals and Sea Otter of the California Coast.* California Fish & Game, vol. 37, 1951.

Bowers, Nathan A., *Cone Bearing Trees of the Pacific Coast.* Palo Alto, Calif., Pacific Books, 1942.

Brower, David, *Not Man Apart.* San Francisco, Sierra Club, 1964.

Brown, Vinson, Weston, Jr., Henry G., *Handbook of California Birds.* Healdsburg, California, Naturegraph Co., 1961.

Buchsbaum, Ralph, *Animals Without Backbones.* University of Chicago Press, 1948.

Carson, Rachel, *The Edge of the Sea.* Boston, Houghton Mifflin, 1955.

——, *The Sea Around Us.* New York, Oxford University Press, 1961.

Cromie, William J., Amos, William H., Allen, Durward L., *Secrets of the Seas.* New York, Canada, Australia, The Reader's Digest Association, 1972.

Dawson, E. Yale, *How to Know the Seaweeds.* Dubuque, Iowa, William C. Brown Co., 1956.

——, *Seashore Plants of Southern California.* Berkeley, Los Angeles, University of California, 1966.

Daugherty, Anita, *Marine Mammals of California.* Sacramento, State of California, The Resources Agency, Dept. of Fish & Game, 1964.

Durrenberger, Robert, *Elements of California Geography.* Palo Alto, National Press Books, 1968.

Emery, K. O., *The Sea off Southern California.* New York, Wiley, 1960.

Fitch, John E., *Offshore Fishes.* State of California, The Resources Agency, Dept. of Fish and Game, Sacramento, California, 1969.

——, *The Pismo Clam.* California Department of Fish & Game, Marine Resources Leaflet No. 1, 1961.

Fry, Jr., Donald H., *Anadromous Fishes of California.* State of California, The Resources Agency, Department of Fish & Game, 1973.

Gotto, R. V., *Marine Animals: Partnerships and Other Associations.* American Elsevier, 1969.

Grinnell, Joseph, Dixon, J. S., Linsdale, J. M., *Fur-Bearing Mammals of California, 2 volumes.* University of California Press, 1937.

Hedgpeth, Joel W., *Seashore Life.* Berkeley, Los Angeles, University of California Press, 1962.

Herald, Earl S., *Living Fishes of the World.* Doubleday, 1961.

Hunt, Charles B., *Physiography of the United States.* San Francisco, W. H. Freeman & Co., 1967.

Ingles, Lloyd Glenn, *Mammals of California and Its Coastal Waters.* Stanford, California, Stanford University Press, 1957.

——, *Mammals of the Pacific States.* Stanford, California, Stanford University Press, 1965.

Jepson, W. L., *A Manual of the Flowering Plants of California.* University of California Press, 1957.

Johnson, Myrtle Elizabeth, Snook, Harry James, *Seashore Animals of the Pacific Coast.* New York, Dover Publications Inc., 1955.

Light, Sol F., and others, *Intertidal Invertebrates of the Central California Coast.* University of California Press, 1957.

Marshall, N. B., *The Life of Fishes.* World, 1966.

Mason, H. L., *A Flora of the Marshes of California.* University of California Press, 1957.

Menard, H. W., *Marine Geology of the Pacific.* New York, McGraw-Hill Book Co., 1964.

Miller, Daniel, J., Gotshall, Dan, Nitsos, Richard, *A Field Guide to Some Common Ocean Sport Fishes of California.* California Department of Fish & Game, 1965.

Miller, Robert C., *The Sea.* Random House, 1966.

Miner, Roy Waldo, *Field Book of Seashore Life.* Putnam, 1950.

Morris, Percy A., *A Field Guide to Shells of the Pacific Coast and Hawaii.* Houghton Mifflin Company Boston, The Riverside Press Cambridge, 1966.

Munz, P. A., *A California Flora.* University of California Press, 1963.

——, *Shore Wildflowers of California, Oregon, & Washington.* University of California Press, 1965.

Orr, Robert T., *Marine Mammals of California.* Berkeley, Los Angeles, London, University of California Press, 1972.

Peattie, Roderick, *The Pacific Coast Ranges.* New York, Vanguard, 1947.

Ricketts, Edward F., Calvin, Jack, *Between Pacific Tides.* Stanford, California, Stanford University Press, 1956.

Shelton, John S., *Geology Illustrated.* San Francisco, London, W. H. Freeman & Co., 1966.

Shepard, Francis P., *The Earth Beneath the Sea.* New York, Atheneum, 1969.
Smith, Lynwood, *Common Seashore Life of Northern California & the Pacific Northwest.* Healdsburg, California, Naturegraph Company, 1962.
Sudworth, George B., *Forest Trees of the Pacific Slope.* New York, Dover Publications, Inc., 1967.
Tinker, Spencer W., *Pacific Seashells.* Charles Tuttle, 1968.
Turner, Charles H., Sexsmith, Jeremy C., *Marine Baits of California.* Sacramento, California, Dept. of Fish and Game, 1965.
Walker, Theodore, J., *Whale Primer, with Special Attention to the California Gray Whale.* Cabrillo Historical Association, 1962.
Yocom, Charles, Dasmann, Ray, *The Pacific Coastal Wildlife Region.* Healdsburg, California, Naturegraph Co., 1965.
Yonge, C. M., *The Sea Shore.* Collins, London, 1949.
Zim, Herbert S., Ingle, Lester, *Seashores.* New York, Golden Press, Western Publishing Company, Inc., 1972.

Guidebooks

Cannon, Raymond, *How to Fish the Pacific Coast.* Menlo Park, California, Lane Publishing Co., 1964.
Doss, Margot Patterson, *Paths of Gold, In and Around the Golden Gate National Recreation Area.* San Francisco, Chronicle Books, 1974.
Elder, Leon, *Free Beaches.* Santa Barbara, California, Capra Press, 1974.
Hayden, Mike, *Guidebook to the Northern California Coast, Volume 1: Highway One.* Los Angeles, The Ward Ritchie Press, 1971.
———, *Guidebook to the Northern California Coast, Volume 2: Humbolt & Del Norte Counties.* Los Angeles, The Ward Ritchie Press, 1971.
Jackson, Ruth A., *Combing the Coast, San Francisco Through Big Sur.* San Francisco, Chronicle Books, 1972.
Sunset, *Travel Guide to Northern California.* Menlo Park, California, Lane Publishing Co., 1975.
———, *Travel Guide to Southern California.* Menlo Park, California, Lane Publishing Co., 1974.

Historical Works

Caughey, John and Laree, *California Heritage.* Los Angeles, Ward Ritchie Press, 1962.
———, *History of the Pacific Coast of North America.* New York, Prentice-Hall, 1938.
Dana, Richard, *Two Years Before the Mast.* Boston, Houghton Mifflin, 1911.
Farquhar, Francis P., *Up and Down California in 1860-1864: The Journal of William H. Brewer.* New Haven, Yale University Press, 1930; Los Angeles & Berkeley, University of California Press, 1966.
Heizer, Robert, and Whipple, M. A., *The California Indians: A Source Book.* Berkeley, University of California Press, 1951.
Mason, Jack, *Early Marin.* Inverness, California, North Shore Books, 1971.
———, *Last Stage for Bolinas.* Inverness, California, North Shore Books, 1973.
Mathes, W. Michael, *Vizcaino and Spanish Expansion in the Pacific Ocean.* San Francisco, California Historical Society, 1968.
McNairn, Jack, and MacMullen, Jerry, *Ships of the Redwood Coast.* Stanford, California, Stanford University Press, 1945.
Newell, Gordon, and Williamson, Joe, *Pacific Lumber Ships.* Seattle, Washington, Superior Publishing Co., 1960.
Ogden, Adele, *The California Sea Otter Trade, 1784-1848.* Berkeley, University of California Press, 1941.
Romoli, Kathleen, *Balboa of Darien: Discoverer of the Pacific.* Garden City, New York, Doubleday & Co., 1953.
Treutlein, Theodore E., *San Francisco Bay: Discovery and Colonization, 1769-1776.* San Francisco, California Historical Society, 1968.

General Interest

Atkeson, Ray, Kentfield, Calvin, *The Pacific Coast.* Chicago, New York, San Francisco, Rand McNally & Co., 1971.
Brokaw, Dennis, Marx, Wesley, *The Pacific Shore, Meeting Place of Man & Nature.* New York, E. P. Dutton & Co., Inc., 1974.
Bronson, William, *How to Kill a Golden State.* Garden City, New York, Doubleday & Company, Inc., 1968.
Camp, Charles L., *Earth Song: A Prologue to History.* Palo Alto, California, American West Publishing Co., 1970.
Cutter, Donald, *The California Coast.* Norman, University of Oklahoma Press, 1969.
Fradkin, Philip L., Stock, Dennis, *California, The Golden Coast.* New York, The Viking Press, 1974.
Gilliam, Harold, *San Francisco Bay.* Garden City, New York, Doubleday & Co., 1957.
———, *Between the Devil & the Deep Blue Bay.* San Francisco, Chronicle Books, 1969.
———, *Island In Time.* San Francisco, Sierra Club, 1962.
Kelley, Don Greame, *Edge of A Continent, The Pacific Coast From Alaska to Baja.* Palo Alto, California, American West Publishing Company, 1971.
Morgan, Neil, *The Pacific States: California, Oregon, Washington.* New York, Time-Life Books, 1967.
———, *Westward Tilt: The American West Today.* New York, Random House, 1963.
Muench, David, Cohen, Jerry, *California Coast.* Chicago, New York, San Francisco, Rand McNally & Company, 1973.
McWilliams, Carey, *Southern California Country.* New York, Duell, Sloan and Pearce, 1946.
Nixon, Stuart, *Redwood Empire.* New York, E. P. Dutton & Co., Inc., 1966.
Reynolds, Robert, *California, Its Coast and Desert.* Portland, Oregon, Charles H. Belding, 1974.
Watkins, T. H., *On the Shore of the Sundown Sea.* San Francisco, New York, Sierra Club, 1973.
Wayburn, Peggy, *Edge of Life.* San Francisco, Sierra Club, 1972.

Index

Old Point Fermin

Piedras Blancas

Point Conception

San Diego

St. George Reef

Old Point Loma

San Luis Obispo